Pat Mesiti

how to
have a
Millionaire
mindset

Foreword by Allan Pease
'From the co-author of Why Men Don't Listen
and Women Can't Read Maps'

How to Have a Millionaire Mindset by Pat Mesiti

This book is dedicated to all our Millionaire Mindset club members around the world.

Published by GOKO Management Pty Ltd in association with Pat Mesiti

GOKO Management Pty Ltd
ACN: 106 523 317
Level 8, 182–186 Blues Point Road
McMahons Point NSW 2060 Sydney Australia
Tel: + 61 2 9922 5334
Fax: + 61 2 9922 5343
Email: info@goko.com.au

Cover Art by Numinos Creative

Printed in Australia by Griffin Press

Distributed to bookshops in Australia by Tower Books,
in New Zealand by Addenda Limited

CONTENTS

FOREWORD

Pat Mesiti has the millionaire mindset and what's even better, he wants you to have a millionaire mindset as well.

Having been involved in personal development all of my life, I was able to study successful people up close. And one thing that stands out like a beacon in the night, one thing that all these successful people possess, is the right mindset.

And I'm often asked, "Is there a way to develop this millionaire mindset? Is there a way to change your thinking from poverty to abundance?" My answer is absolutely! And in this book, Pat gives you the keys to unlocking the fortune that lies hidden inside your mind.

Pat has harnessed the power of mindset and in this book he sets it out for you in straightforward language what needs to be done. His life is dedicated to unlocking the potential inside of people, and opening up their minds to a more rewarding, fulfilling and prosperous future.

Pat walks his talk. From meagre beginnings in the back streets of working–class Sydney, to world–renowned author and speaker, Pat lives the life that most people would envy. He proves that anyone, from anywhere, can truly be successful no matter what their past or where they began.

In this book Pat shares with you his life… the good, the bad, and the ugly. He will share with you how he discovered abundance and how, with the right kind of thinking, you can claim your share of riches too.

This book is all about change, and how you can create your own future full of riches.

Once you acquire the power of the millionaire mindset, you'll be free of worry and doubt. You'll no longer have to wonder about your future. You'll be able to clearly map out a future full of abundance, all by using your own mind.

As you read this book, take note of the coach's advice, trust him when he tells you to think differently, and immediately follow his directions at the end of each chapter. And then be ready for the miraculous transformation that happens in your life.

The mindset you have determines your success, it's that simple yet that profound. It stands to reason that when you develop a winning, millionaire mindset, it will take you closer to your dreams.

If you're looking for a resource that will get you into the ballpark, that will have you hitting home runs, the book in your hands can take you there.

Begin this journey now with an open mind and reap the rewards on offer. This is the start of a new beginning. Step forward and claim your new future full of riches and abundance. Your mind holds the answers to achieving anything you want. And this book will show you how.

Allan Pease
Author of 8 No.1 bestsellers

INTRODUCTION

I'm on a mission to help make people rich. And to do that, I mess with people's minds. That's why I've written this book. You may wonder what a book about mindsets has to do with you! Well it's very simple: we all need to have the right kind of mindset to achieve wealth and prosperity. You see, prosperity isn't about money, it's about mindsets. Change your mindset, and you can change your world.

How many times have you read about a person who has won a fortune in the lottery and a few years later is back on poverty street with nothing left of their winnings? I remember reading about a man in the USA who won $276 million in a lottery and lost it all in just two years. (He must have had a pretty big couple of years!) World champion boxer Mike Tyson earned about $400 million over the course of his career and yet today he is bankrupt. How does that sort of thing happen? How do you lose that much money? I'll tell you how: the same way you lose $1,000 or $10,000. You see, it's not about the money. It has a lot to do with your mindset. You cannot move to another level in your life with the same mindset you have right now. Here's the key to moving to another level: change your mindset!

We need to shift our thinking if our life is going to change. Let me ask you a question: if you want your life to prosper, will the same level of thinking that you currently have be good enough to get you to another level? The answer is: No! Is it possible to change your thinking? Yes!

A few years ago, I was in New York City and I'd been asked to speak as part of a street program run by one of the local communities. We had a few counsellors and a salsa band there and, as the program got underway, I wondered what I should speak about. The streets were dark and there were a few crack houses close by. There was evidence of violence everywhere. When it came time for me to speak, I stood up and spoke on the topic 'When Love Comes to Town'. I spoke about the power of love and I shared my story. I talked about where I had come from and what I understood to be love: love is gentle, love is kind, love is patient, love doesn't rejoice in doing wrong, love doesn't hold grudges...

My friend Danny, who was running the program, said to me, "Pat, give an invitation to people to come forward off the street if they want help and if they want food because we want to help them!"

I turned and said to him, "Danny, there's no one here!" Danny, who is Puerto Rican, said to me, "This is my town! I know my people! Just do it!"

"Okay!" I replied. (I've learned not to mess with Puerto Ricans!)

So I invited people to come forward if they needed help. All of a sudden, people started coming out of the crack houses pushing their trollies. It looked like a scene from Michael Jackson's Thriller video! As I was standing there, a guy came up to me and he stunk of booze and vomit (which is kind of like Old Spice aftershave!). This man's hair was all matted together. As he came closer I could see through his beard lesions all over his face, the result of HIV infection. He stunk unbelievably.

He whispered to me in a husky voice, "Hey! You talk about love... Do you love me?"

I took two steps back and said, "Yeah, I love you."

He said to me, "If you love me, you hug me!"

A little voice inside me that I've come to know said to me, "Hug him!"

"You hug him!" I replied.

"I would," said the inner voice, "but I need someone to hug through and you happen to be the closest thing that I know."

I reached out and said, "What's your name?"

"Hector," he said.

I said, "Hector, come here!"

He stepped forward and fell into my arms. He began to sob. I began to sob. I realised that I couldn't smell him anymore, but I could feel his pain. Through tears he began to tell me what had happened to him that morning.

"I was going through the trash this morning and I found an old cup of coffee," he said. "Something came over me and I prayed, 'God, if you're there, get someone to hug me today. I've never been hugged'."

I said, "Hector, do you realise you are dying of HIV?"

"What is that?" he asked.

LOVE CAME TO TOWN!

Well, we welcomed Hector into that community and, sure enough, love came to town! We cleaned him up and got him some work.

I went back to that community in New York two years later and I said to my friend Danny, "Hey, Danny! Where's Hector?"

"Hector is dead, man!" he said.

I was devastated. I had been so looking forward to seeing Hector. Danny saw the look on my face and whacked me. (Puerto Ricans have no compassion!)

"Hey, Mr Motivation!" he said. "What's your problem?"

"The man's dead!" I said, tears welling in my eyes.

"Ah," he said. "So you got a philosophical problem, man? Sometimes there is something far greater than just breathing air. Come here with me!" he said to me.

He took me to a back room of the community facility where he worked. In that room I saw about 150 people – old people, young people, black people, and white people. Some of them had headsets on their heads and they were peering at television screens, computer screens and laptop screens...all these people were working!

"Hey, everybody look at me!" Danny shouted.

Everyone turned around to look at Danny.

He pointed at one of them and said, "You! Get up! Tell Pat your story!"

This man stood up and said, "My name is Eduardo. I was a gang member, man. I would pop people for $20. Hector came into my life!"

Danny pointed to a woman. She stood up and said, "My name is Cindy. I was a street worker. I used to waste my life. I was a mainline junkie. Look, man! Hector came into my life!"

Danny pointed to someone else who also stood up. "My name is Ricardo. I also used to do drugs. Hector came into my life!"

Another man stood up. "My name is Shaque. (Black guys always have the cool names!) I used to pop guys. I used to deal drugs. That was my $100,000 corner, man. Hector came into my life!"

WE HAVE HEALTHY BODIES, BUT WE'VE GOT VIRUSES IN OUR MINDS

One after the other, people stood up and told me how Hector came into their life. Danny turned to me and said, "Sometimes the wealthiest man on the planet is the one who leaves behind a legacy for others." You see, Hector had spent the last days of his life giving to others what had been given to him: love and a second chance at building a better life.

I suddenly realised something. The only reason why Hector was able to impact all these lives was because no one had told him he couldn't. He had a virus in his body, but he didn't have one in his mind. The problem with a lot of us is that we have healthy bodies, but we've got viruses in our minds. My friend, I want to help you change that!

A little while ago I was invited to speak at a financial planning seminar and at this seminar was a very prominent sportsman. He came up to me after I had spoken and said, "I enjoyed what you said. But I want to ask you something. I want to be a great football player! Can you help me?"

I looked at him and I said, "Don't you mean that you want to be a great person?"

He said, "Yeah, that's right. I want to be a great player. I want to be recognised as one of the legends of the game!"

I said to him, "Okay, how would you rate yourself on a scale from one to 10 as a player and as a person?" You see, I look at the whole person, and I wanted him to do the same. My friend, you can't compartmentalise the different facets of your life.

So he replied, "I reckon I'm an eight."

I said, "I reckon you're a six. You can still go up a few notches."

He said to me, "Yeah, okay. I'm a six."

YOUR CURRENT MINDSET WON'T GET YOU TO THE NEXT LEVEL

Now, I knew he was already a good player, but he wanted to go up another level. I also knew that the same effort, the same level of commitment, and the same level of discipline that he had applied up to that point in his life would not get him to a level eight on the scale.

I said to him, "Now, you said you want to be great. Alright, I'm prepared to take you on board on this condition. Here's what I want you to do. First, I want you to go to bed earlier at night. Second, no going out boozing six nights a week. Third, I want you to do extra training. Fourth, stick to one girlfriend. On top of that, I want you to read some books. Get some material to build you on the inside. Every single day I want you to give yourself to some personal development as a person."

Here's the problem with most of us: we work harder on our jobs than we do on ourselves and that's why most people stay broke. This player wanted to work harder on his game, but I wanted him to work harder on his person.

This football player shook his head and said, "I can't do it!"

"Then stay average!" I said. You see, if you want to be great, you've got to do what great people do!

At one level, Mike Tyson was an incredible achiever. He had a dream, he had goals, and he pursued them with great determination and with great success. You might have a dream and hit every goal you set for yourself too, but a dream in and of itself is not enough. Unless you are able to change your mindset to think how wealthy people think — to think with a millionaire mindset — you won't achieve sustainable prosperity. Like lottery winners, you may gain a large sum of money next week, but without a millionaire mindset, it may soon disappear. The bottom line is that your income won't keep you where your mindset can't hold you.

A story is told of a Texan who walked into a church office one day and said to the secretary, "Honey, I'd like to speak to the chief hog in the trough."

"I beg your pardon!" she responded. "Are you referring to our Senior Minister?"

"That's right, honey," he said. "I want to speak to the chief hog in the trough."

She looked him in the eye and said, "He's a man of integrity, he's a man of character, he's a man of the Scriptures, and he's a man above reproach. How dare you speak about him in such a fashion!"

"Oh, honey," he said. "I'm sorry. I have a cheque here for a million dollars that I wanted to give him for the church building fund."

She immediately turned around and said, "Hang on a minute. I think I see the big fat pig coming right now."

You see, this church secretary had an instant change in mindset.

My friend, motivational speaker Brian Willersdorf, tells the story of a Baptist minister whose friend strode up to him one day and said, "Look, my dog's sick. Could you pray for my dog?"

The minister responded, "Buddy, we're Baptists. We pray for people, we don't do dogs. But I do know a good Catholic priest who could help you."

The man looked at the minister and said, "Well, what's his name?"

"His name is Father McKenzie," said the minister.

"Well, would you please give Father McKenzie this cheque for $20,000 and thank him for praying for my dog when he does?"

Quick as a flash the Baptist minister replied, "Oh, you didn't tell me it was a Baptist dog!"

It's amazing how quickly we can change our mindsets when under pressure.

IF YOU LEARN TO THINK DIFFERENTLY, YOU WILL START TO SEE BETTER RESULTS

Adolf Hitler once said, "What luck for rulers that men do not think." Unfortunately, his legacy proves his point. My friend, if you learn to think differently, you will start to see better results in your personal and professional life.

Let me explain with another illustration. America has blessed many nations with great franchises. One of the incredible franchises that has been shipped to Australian shores is the great Krispy Kreme Doughnuts franchise. The reason I love Krispy Kreme donuts is because they are the only low calorie donut in the world...not! Seriously, I love Krispy Kreme donuts and every chance I get to eat their donuts, I'm in.

I've discovered that there is a Krispy Kreme franchise at Sydney Airport. In my line of work I travel a lot. Generally I leave for the airport about 45 minutes earlier than I need to, just in case my plane leaves earlier (at least that's what I tell my wife). The real reason I get to the airport early is so I can enjoy a Krispy Kreme donut and a cup of coffee.

One day I was at a Krispy Kreme shop and there was a guy there with his two little girls. I was standing in line behind them waiting to be served. The girls were looking in eager anticipation at all the choices available in the donut cabinet. Watching these cute little girls made me feel a little wistful because they reminded me of when my own two daughters were little.

As I was admiring this charming little scene unfold in front of me, I heard the father say to his daughters, "Girls, you can have any donuts you like, except for the ones on the top shelf."

Now, you and I and everybody else in the world know that the donuts those little girls wanted were...You guessed it, on the top shelf!

On the top shelf were the most expensive donuts, but they were only about 20 or 30 cents more than the other donuts. I could see these two little girls eagerly looking at the top shelf donuts. They were obviously disappointed at the news that the top shelf was off limits. I quietly went over to the father who was puffing on a cigarette and handed him $20. (I made sure that I did it in such a way that it would not embarrass him.)

"Here, sir, buy the girls the donuts on the top shelf," I said to him.

"Who are you?" he asked me, surprised.

"I'm the answer to your children's prayer," I replied. "Buddy, I teach people to prosper. I encourage people to invest not just in things, but in memories. It's the greatest thing you can give your children. Buy the girls a donut from the top shelf. An extra 30 cents isn't going to make you broke."

DO YOU HAVE A POVERTY MINDSET OR A PROSPERITY MINDSET?

This man did not have what I call a 'millionaire mindset'. He had a poverty mindset that made him automatically think, "I can't afford the most expensive donuts." And by telling his daughters that they couldn't have the donuts on the top shelf, he was indoctrinating them with the same mindset. Even worse is the possibility that these two delightful little girls could have gone away from that shop thinking, "We don't deserve the best. We're not good enough to have really nice things. We have to settle for second best." Even something as simple as buying a donut can have a critical impact on the mindset of our children.

The problem here was not the donuts. The problem was a mindset. How did I know that it was a mindset issue and not a case of genuinely not having enough money? Well, to begin with, I noticed that the man was smoking a cigarette. Cigarettes cost about $10 a packet and he probably smokes a packet a day. That's about $70 a week or $3,640 a year. Even if he was only smoking a couple of packets a week, it's still a lot of money compared to the few extra cents it would have cost him for a couple of 'top shelf' donuts.

This father had a choice: he could invest in mind viruses or he could invest in memories. He could create a mindset in his daughters that would potentially limit their future prosperity or he could begin to build a mindset in them by which they would grow up believing that they have unlimited potential. He could spend his money on cigarettes and watch it go up in smoke or he could invest his small change in the future prosperity of his two delightful little children. After the man ordered and paid for his 'top shelf' donuts, one of the little girls looked at me and smiled. "Thanks, mister," she said. Personally, I'd pay $20 any day to see a smile like that!

EVERY SO OFTEN DETERMINE TO GO UP A NOTCH

I want to encourage you that it's okay to eat from the top shelf. Now, you don't have to go for the top shelf all the time. You don't have to stay at the luxury Palazzo Versace Hotel, and you don't have to wear a Rolex watch. I'm not suggesting that you progress from McDonald's to restaurants that serve $70–a–plate meals. And I'm not suggesting that every time you make a purchase that you get into debt. Not at all! Simply learn to grow. Take it gradually. Recognise that it's a process. Start somewhere and expand your life in stages. Every so often when you buy something, determine to go up a notch; stretch yourself a little bit. Men, when you take your wife or your girlfriend out to a restaurant, take her to a restaurant that's just a little nicer than the ones you've been to before. Make the sacrifice and enjoy it.

One of my great friends is a businessman involved in a large coffee franchise. He was with me the first time I spent over $80 on a tie. Now, I like nice ties. (What can I say? I'm Italian. I can't help it!) But I'd never before spent more than $20 on a tie. I was looking at two ties — one was $80 and the other was $90. The idea of buying an $80 tie was quite a stretch for me, but my friend, seeing that I really preferred the $90 tie, said to me, "Go on, Pat. Get the $90 one. Go up a level. It's not going to affect your entire income." My friend challenged my mindset.

What kind of mindset do you have when it comes to wealth, money and prosperity? Do you have a millionaire mindset or a poverty mindset? Are you a 'top shelf' kind of person or a 'bottom shelf' kind of person? Is prosperity something that only happens to other people? Is prosperity something you'd love to have, but can only dream about?

The word 'prosperity' comes from the Latin word *prosperare,* which means 'to succeed'. The word 'prosper' means 'to be fortunate, to bloom, to flourish, to progress, to succeed and to thrive'. To me, prosperity means wealth, well being, affluence, influence, success, and a good life. In all these meanings there is a connotation of advancement. My belief is that every one of us is meant to enjoy a prosperous life. We were never meant to only exist. We are born to live life wonderfully and amazingly! Our lives are meant to advance!

How many times in your life have you dreamed about what it would be like to be wealthy? Many people spend their whole lives wishing they had more money, but they never do anything about it. (By the way, buying a weekly lotto ticket doesn't count!) The truth is, you can live a more prosperous life if you are prepared to make some changes in your life.

The first place in which change needs to happen is in your mind. Before you can become a millionaire, you need to develop the mindset of a millionaire. This book is all about helping you to shift your thinking from a poverty mindset to a millionaire mindset. It isn't just about financial prosperity, it's also about mental and emotional wealth; it's about abundance and success in every area of your life. Prosperity definitely includes financial wealth, but it should never be limited to this. Prosperity is something that affects your whole life.

As we journey through the pages of this book, I want to be your coach. People have coaches for a lot of reasons, but often we neglect some of the most important reasons. Prosperity is an important part of life. My goal is to lead you into a new way of thinking, to help you to think logically, not just emotionally; to help you understand the difference between millionaire thinking and poverty thinking. I want you to become a 'top shelf' donut kind of person!

YOU HAVE TO DECIDE THAT YOU'RE GOING TO BE A WEALTHY PERSON

Generally speaking, genuine prosperity does not happen by accident. It takes a decision on our part to become prosperous. We have to be committed to prosperity. If you're not fully committed to becoming prosperous, then you can't blame anybody or anything else for your lack of prosperity. Your upbringing, your job, your organisation, your education are not responsible for your prosperity. If you want to prosper, then there's only one person that matters — you! You have to decide that you are going to be a wealthy person.

As we work our way through this book, my aim is to help you to begin to think differently. First, you have to think differently about yourself. You need to start seeing yourself as a person who can prosper. You may need to change some ingrained thinking patterns, or perhaps you'll need to overcome negative mindsets that have developed as a result of past experiences. You might also need to change how you think about wealth and money.

Second, you have to change your thinking about your future. Your future is not predetermined. Rather, you create your future by the decisions and choices you make today. What you need is a dream, a clear vision of the future you want to create for yourself.

Finally, you may need to change the way you think about other people. Instead of seeing others as being in competition with us, or as obstacles around which we need to negotiate on our way to personal success, we need to see other people as part of the key to our own success. Other people need to become the ultimate purpose for our prosperity. What do I mean by this? Simply this: our primary reason for pursuing prosperity has to be so that we can do something to make life better, not just for ourselves, but for others as well.

Are you ready for a mind shift? Are you willing to get rid of thought patterns, ideas about yourself and your world, and mindsets about money and wealth that have kept you contained? Are you willing to kick out those thought patterns, ideas and mindsets that have prevented you from stepping into the truly prosperous life that you were born for and that is waiting to be discovered? Do you want to have a millionaire mindset? Then let's get started!

CHAPTER 1

mind viruses

I'm sick and tired of the mind viruses that are crippling our nation and our people! We're becoming a nation of whingers. People want to change everything around them. "If I could only live in a better suburb!" they say. "If my children could only attend a better school! If I could only get a better paying job!"

Some of us want the economy to change. Some of us want the weather to change. For some people there's too much rain. For others there's not enough rain. Some people don't like the summer and others don't like the winter. My friend, you can't change the economy, you can't change the weather, and you can't change the seasons. The answer to your problems is not out there, it's in your thinking, it's in your mindset.

A young man by the name of Danny came to the drug rehabilitation centre I was running a few years ago. Now, Danny used to drink lime green cordial straight from the bottle. One day he saw someone mixing water with lime green cordial.

"What are you doing?" he challenged. "You're a real tight wad!"

Surprised, the man turned to Danny and said, "Danny, let me tell you something. You're not supposed to drink cordial straight from the bottle."

Do you know why Danny drank lime green cordial straight from the bottle? Because he didn't know any better. Many of us are like Danny. We want a better life. We want to be prosperous. We want to improve our relationships. But we're going about it the wrong way and we just don't know any better! The first thing you've got to do is shift your mindset, and the next thing you've got to do is get rid of some of your viruses.

The answer to your problems is not out there, it's in your thinking, it's in your mindset.

There are many viruses out there that infect our minds. These viruses are reflected as attitudes and thought patterns that have entered our minds quietly and unobtrusively over the years. Many of them we catch during our childhood. When we're young, we're vulnerable and teachable, and we absorb both good and bad mindsets because we don't know any better.

Many of these viruses affect the way we think about money and success. If you catch these viruses, they limit your opportunities for success because they cause you to see everything as negative, as threats, and as problems.

Let me illustrate. I love receiving bills! You may think I have a problem. But it's true! I love bills. Too many people shake in their boots when a bill arrives in the mail. If you're one of those people, you need to shift your mindset about bills. Do you know what bills mean to me? They mean that I am decreasing my liabilities and I am increasing my assets! Now there's a real mindset shift! You see, for many of you your reaction to bills shows you have a mind virus about bills.

You can quickly recognise mind viruses in other people by the way they react to things, like other people's success. You can easily test whether someone has a mind virus by asking them questions. For instance, ladies could try this on their men: next time you go shopping for a dress, ask your husband or boyfriend to go with you. When you see a really expensive dress, tell your husband or boyfriend, "I've chosen this one! Isn't it nice!" Then watch for his reaction, because what comes out of his mouth will reveal whether he has a mind virus.

You can also test whether your friends have a mind virus. Tell a friend about a successful CEO of a well known corporation who recently resigned and was given a multimillion dollar hand–out...and wait for your friend's response.

Talk to a colleague about how wealthy business people seem to be better than most at clever tax avoidance strategies...

Next time you are at the hairdressers, talk about how so many celebrities end up divorced within a few short years...

Talk to your work mates about network marketing...

Tell your parents you're giving up your job to pursue your dream of becoming a musician in a rock band...

THIRTY–ONE EXAMPLES OF MIND VIRUSES

Here are just 31 mind viruses I've spotted, some of which you too may have caught over the years:

1. Money doesn't grow on trees!
2. I'm not made of money!
3. We'd never be able to afford that!
4. It's not whether you win or lose, it's whether you had fun that matters! (Generally people say that to someone who has just lost.)
5. The rich get richer, the poor get poorer, and the middle class go shopping!
6. Wogs get all the good jobs!
7. I didn't have it easy as a kid, so why should you?
8. No one ever gave me a free lunch!
9. Money ruined my marriage! (No it didn't — you did it all by yourself!)
10. Money made him greedy! (No it didn't — money magnified what he already was!)
11. You mustn't give people false hope!
12. Who do you think you are...better than me?!
13. The rich keep all the secrets to themselves!
14. Welcome to my humble home!
15. I'm just an average Aussie battler! (There's nothing Aussie about being a battler!)

16. No one in our family ever amounted to much!

17. Don't rock the boat!

18. Money is the root of all evil! (No it isn't — the love of money is the root of all evil!)

19. I could never wear that! I could never drive that! I could never live there!

20. Money won't make you happy! (Well, neither will being broke!)

21. Life wasn't meant to be easy! (Don't try to make life easy — try to make life better!)

22. Get an education so you can get a good job! In fact, get a government job or a job at the bank!

23. That child has Attention Deficit Disorder! (Not necessarily — if they're anything like me, they may just need to be taught some discipline or taught boundaries or taught to focus...Too often we're quick to medicate the magic out of children.)

24. You've got to acknowledge your strengths, but focus on your weaknesses! (No, you will never build prosperity out of your weaknesses, you'll only build prosperity out of your strengths.)

25. I wonder how many people he had to walk over to get to where he is?

26. I bet she's never done a hard day's work in her life!

27. That's impossible! It can't be done!

28. You don't have what it takes!

29. It's been tried before. What makes you think you can succeed where others have failed?

30. You're being too ambitious!

31. We pay too much tax!

PEOPLE WHO HAVE BEEN FAMOUSLY CAUGHT OUT BY MIND VIRUSES

Now, look at what happens when you let a mind virus affect your judgement. These people obviously had a virus:

> *"There is no reason anyone would want a computer in their home!"*
> – Kenneth Olsen, President and Founder of Digital Equipment

Corporation (1977).

"Computers in the future may perhaps only weigh 1.5 ton." – *Popular Mechanics* forecasting the development of computer technology (1949).

"The horse is here to stay, but automobiles are only a passing novelty." – The President of Michigan Savings Bank advising Horace H. Rackham (Henry Ford's lawyer) not to invest in the Ford Motor Company in 1903. Rackham ignored the advice, bought $5,000 worth of stock, and sold it several years later for $12.5 million.

"Man will never reach the moon, regardless of all the future scientific advances." – Dr. Lee de Forest, inventor of the vacuum tube and the father of radio (1967).

"Television won't be able to hold onto any market it catches after the first six months. People will soon get tired of staring at a plywood box every night." – Darryl F. Zanuck, head of 20th Century Fox (1946).

"I have no political ambitions for myself or my children." – Joseph P. Kennedy (1936).

"What use could this company make of an electrical toy?" – Western Union President William Orton rejecting Alexander Graham Bell's offer to sell his struggling telephone company to Western Union for $100,000. (1876)

"I confess that in 1901 I said to my brother Orville that man would not fly for 50 years. Ever since I have distrusted myself and avoided all predictions." – Wilbur Wright, US aviation pioneer (1908).

"Who the hell wants to hear actors talk?" – Harry M. Warner of Warner Brothers Studios (1927).

THE MYTH OF THE AUSSIE BATTLER

One of the mind viruses that pervades the Australian culture is the myth of the 'Aussie battler'. I have to admit that this is one of my pet hates. The whole Aussie battler concept is nothing more than a negative mindset that keeps people suppressed and contained. It discourages entrepreneurship and it is a misnomer.

There's nothing Australian about being a battler. Australians are meant to be achievers, not battlers. There's nothing 'battler' about the Anzacs, Howard Florey, Ian Thorpe, Evonne Goolagong, Don Bradman, the 800 horsemen who liberated Beersheba (probably for the beer!) or any other of our great Australians who have made their mark on the world over the past two centuries. Our nation is not a nation of battlers.

The Aussie battler label creates a particular mindset that says that if you are a true Aussie, then you must be doing it tough and you're always going to be the underdog. This ridiculous notion of the Aussie battler is responsible for centuries of Australians who have lived far beneath their potential level of prosperity.

A few years ago, the Australian Government introduced a financial support system for families with children. They were giving all families — those they love to call 'average Aussie battlers' — a certain amount of money each month for family support. I immediately rang the government department that administered the payments and refused to accept the money. Why? Because I am not an Aussie battler and I refuse to allow that mindset any space in my life. I do not want to see myself as a battler. I am a winner, a victor, a high achiever, and a walking prosperity machine.

CHALLENGE

My friend, you are not an Aussie battler! If your mindset is telling you, "I'm a battler! Things are tight! I can't afford that!", then your life will gravitate towards that mindset and your behaviour will reflect that mindset. You need to realise that you can never be prosperous if the dominant mindset that governs your life and actions is one of disbelief, lack and negativity. Recognise it as a mind virus and fight to reject it.

We aren't Aussie battlers, we're Aussie winners and proud of it!

CHAPTER 2

get started

Think about your life for a moment. How satisfied are you with the level of prosperity in your life right now? Do you have a strong desire to be more prosperous? Or are you content with where you're at? If you are totally satisfied with the level of prosperity in your life right now, then you have no incentive to change. Perhaps you would like to be more wealthy but have resigned yourself to the 'fact' that 'this is as good as it's ever going to get' for you. In other words, your level of discontent is not sufficient enough to motivate you to strive for change.

Before there can be any change in your life, there has to be an acknowledgement that things are not as good as they could or should be. Then there has to be a resolution to do something about the level of prosperity in your life. Change starts with a decision to do something about a situation with which we are dissatisfied. In order to increase prosperity, there needs to be some serious discontent in your life. There will be no prosperity without discontent about where you are versus where you want to be. Contentment means containment. As soon as you become content with the level of prosperity in your life, you have set the limits of your prosperity.

My friend, you and I were never meant to be contained. You and I were created with unlimited capacity. But our capacity for increase depends on our level of discontent. This doesn't mean that you should live life in a constant state of frustration, dissatisfaction and disappointment, never being able to enjoy or appreciate what you have. No, like the athlete who is always pursuing his or her next 'personal best', there should always be a desire in us to grow, to increase, and to go one level better than we've ever been able to achieve so far. As the famous banker David Rockefeller once observed, "If necessity is the mother of invention, discontent is the father of progress."

Discontent takes us beyond desire to a place where action becomes not simply an option but an imperative. If prosperity is only an option to you, you will never achieve it. To get started on the path to increased prosperity, prosperity needs to become not merely an option but a lifestyle to which you are totally committed. It is a lifestyle that affects every area of your world — your thinking, your relationships, your health, and, of course, your finances. It's a lifestyle that transforms not just your outer world, but also who you are as a person. Desire alone is not enough. It takes discontent and focus to advance. It requires a willingness to make some sacrifices, to change the way we think and live. It takes a serious commitment to address areas of your life that are not working for you, even if it means you have to become uncomfortable. You will never become the person you want to be by remaining just as you are.

WE WILL NEVER CHANGE WHAT WE CONSISTENTLY TOLERATE

Are you sick of remaining stuck at your current level of prosperity? Are you frustrated with the amount of lack in your life? Are you tolerating a small-thinking mindset? What happens is this: we tolerate, then we navigate. What do I mean by this? When we tolerate things in our life that hold us back, we find ourselves constantly having to navigate around those things by making excuses for being the way we are. But if we don't tolerate, then we will no longer navigate. Instead, we will instigate. We will instigate new habits, new behaviours and new ways of thinking in our lives. Remember, we will never change what we consistently tolerate.

Some people are always complaining about their lives. They say, "I hate being broke!", "My staff are always late!", "I'm sick of being overweight!", "I hate being unhealthy!", "I don't like my bad temper!", and "I don't like my bad spending habits!" How often do you catch yourself saying statements like that? As much as you might say how much you hate certain things in your life, the truth is you don't really hate them enough, because if you really hated these things, you wouldn't tolerate them.

Remember, we will never change what we consistently tolerate.

Let me give you a little illustration of what I mean. I don't like beetroot. In fact, I hate beetroot with a passion. I think the worst kind of eternal punishment would be having to eat nothing but beetroot for the rest of my life. So, because I don't like it, I don't eat it. Because I don't like it, I don't tolerate it. I don't tolerate it in a hamburger. I don't tolerate it in a salad. I simply refuse to have beetroot in my life. If a smoker says to me, "I hate smoking", my reply is, "Then why do you smoke? If you really hated it, you wouldn't tolerate it — you wouldn't smoke!" When we really hate something, we refuse to tolerate it.

YOUR LEVEL OF DISCONTENT WILL FINALLY GIVE IN TO CHANGE

Prosperity is hindered by what you won't give up. Here is another illustration. A friend of mine was living in a run–down part of town. It was a government housing commission area where all the houses were painted canary yellow. One day a man turned up at his house and gave it a fresh coat of canary yellow paint. My friend hated the colour of his house. He didn't like living in that area, but he had tolerated it for many years. But on the day that man came and painted his house canary yellow, he finally decided he'd had enough. His level of discontent finally got to a point where putting up with the status quo was no longer an acceptable option. He decided he would not allow himself to continue to be contained by his upbringing. He said to his wife, "We will never have our house painted canary yellow again!"

Then he began to make some changes. He decided to take hold of a small business opportunity that became available to him. He stopped spending lazy days in front of the television flicking from channel to channel. He stopped watching sports on television every day. He began to work hard at his new, small home–based business. Today, my friend lives in a ten–bedroom house with a pool. He has a view of the water in one of the most prestigious beachfront areas in Australia. Realising he had a choice, he stopped tolerating circumstances that he wasn't happy with, and he began to instigate change. As a result, he no longer lives in a canary yellow house.

You will never change what you are constantly prepared to tolerate. One of my favourite quotes is, "Change is not change until something changes." The longer you tolerate lack, inconsistency, laziness, inactivity and bad habits in your life, the longer you are delaying your prosperity. Constant change is a permanent condition in the life of any successful person. Warren Bennis of the Leadership Institute said this: "In life, change is inevitable; in business, it is vital." Steven Covey, author of *The 7 Habits of Highly Effective People,* said, "If you keep doing what you're doing, you'll keep getting what you're getting!" I would add to his statement, "So if you don't like what you're getting, don't tolerate it...change it!"

HABIT BREAKING IS A PREREQUISITE FOR CHANGE AND RENEWAL

The first step towards becoming more prosperous is to make a decision and declare, "I am not staying here any longer!" My friend in the canary yellow house hit a crisis point. If the desire for something greater doesn't drive you to change, then a crisis generally will. Robert H. Waterman, co–author of *In Search of Excellence,* says, "Habit breaking is a prerequisite for change and renewal. It needs more than a simple decision. It takes motivation, desire and will."

The millionaire mindset is all about prosperity. Remember, the word 'prosperity' means 'to bloom, to flourish, to progress, to succeed and to thrive'. It is all about continual advancement in every area of your life. If you ever think you have finally arrived at where you want to be in life, then you have reached the end of your prosperity. Prosperity must be seen as a journey, not a destination. The fact is that you never actually arrive at prosperity. It involves a continual evolvement of your mind, your will, your emotions, your relationships, your wealth, and every other area of your life.

In 1870 a man called Russell H. Conwell was riding a camel caravan along the valley between the Tigris and Euphrates Rivers in Mesopotamia when one of the guides began to entertain a group of American tourists with some local tales. The then 27–year–old Conwell was deeply impressed by the story of a rich Persian farmer named Ali Hafed. One day Ali heard a Buddhist priest speaking about mythical diamond fields in some faraway land. Ali decided to give up his own fruitful lands to go and search for this immense wealth. For many years Ali Hafed travelled far and wide. He grew old and poor and eventually died far from home, a disillusioned and broke old man. Tragically, soon after his death, acres of fabulous diamonds were found on Ali Hafed's own land. The story of Ali Hafed had a huge impact on Conwell and formed in his mind a great truth that he would live by for the rest of his life: "Your diamonds are not in faraway mountains or in distant seas; they are in your own backyard if you will but dig for them."

The exciting truth in all this is that the starting point of the quest for a millionaire mindset is wherever you are right now. No matter who you are, or what you know or don't know about money and wealth, or what your current circumstances are, or what has happened to you in the past, if you simply make a firm decision today to do something to change your world, then you are at the starting point of seeing increase and prosperity in your life.

CHALLENGE

Let me challenge you to do just that. Make a decision to change. Decide that 'good enough' is no longer good enough for you. Commit yourself to pursue the best in every area of your life, to become the person you were born to be. You're now at the starting line of your journey to develop a millionaire mindset.

CHAPTER 3

change begins in your mind

According to Mark Hansen and Robert Allen, authors of *The One Minute Millionaire*, someone becomes a millionaire somewhere every 60 seconds. Why can't that be you? Sometimes it takes a lifetime to make a million dollars; sometimes it can take just a few years. But no matter how long the first million might be in coming, it always starts with a thought process, a change of mindset. We need to ensure that our inner world and our outer world are in sync. Most people want to change their outer world, but they fail to address the need to change their inner world.

All of us have internal blockages to prosperity that we need to deal with before we will see significant external change. There is a verse in the Bible that says, "I pray that you may prosper in all things and be in health, just as your soul prospers."[1] The Greek word here is *psuche*, translated as 'soul', from which we get the word 'psyche', which refers to the mind. This verse succinctly expresses the idea that there is a link between the prosperity of the mind and prosperity in "all things".

Change begins in the mind. The mind is like a filter through which we interpret the world and our own experiences and through which we form our beliefs, attitudes and understanding of the nature of 'reality'. No two people see a single situation the same way. The classic illustration of

[1] 3 John 2 (New King James Version)

this is the difference between the person who sees a glass of water as half empty and the one who sees the same glass as half full — same glass, different perspectives. Why the difference? Because the minds of the two observers are filtering the information they are receiving about the glass differently. We would label the first person as a pessimist and the second as an optimist.

WEALTH IS MORE ABOUT INVESTING THAN IT IS ABOUT SPENDING

But more important than categorising the different points of view is the need to understand why each of these two people sees things the way they do. To begin with, one person is putting water into the glass while the other is taking it out. A millionaire mindset sees that wealth is more about investing in something than it is about spending. To continue with the water metaphor, do you see wealth in your life as a reservoir that is gradually running dry? Or do you see it as an endless spring that is continually brimming over?

In order to begin the process of shifting the way you think and changing your mindset, you first need to understand how your mind works as a filter and why it filters things the way it does. This will lead you to an understanding of why you need to change the way you think and the way you view the world. I'm not saying that we all need to get into some kind of deep psychotherapeutic experience. It's simply a matter of developing a basic understanding of why we think the way we do. What is shaping or has shaped your thinking and your worldview? For example, how do you view money? When contemplating a purchase, does your mind naturally go to a 'can't afford it' or a 'too expensive' mindset?

> *Wealth is more about investing in something than it is about spending.*

A friend of mine who is quite wealthy was once shopping for a ring for his wife. He was accompanied by one of his mentors. He saw a stunning ring priced at $26,000 and considered buying it. Although he could easily afford it, he decided that this was too much to pay for a ring. "I don't need to spend that much," he reasoned. "My wife will still be impressed by a much less expensive ring." His mentor looked at him. "Stay average then," he said. He could see that my friend had a mindset issue that needed to be challenged. Despite his affluence, he was retreating into a poverty mindset. His mindset was really no different to that of the man at the Krispy Kreme counter. It's not a matter of how much money you do or do not have, it's about whether or not you have a millionaire mindset.

Did you grow up in a home where all you ever heard from your parents were expressions like "We're not made of money!" or "Money doesn't grow on trees!"? Or perhaps your view of money is even more severe; maybe you grew up hearing statements like "Money is the root of all evil!" or "Money ruined my marriage!"

BEFORE YOU CAN TRULY PROSPER YOU NEED TO CHANGE YOUR MINDSET

If your mindset is that money is always incredibly hard to come by, or that money is somehow inherently evil, then before you can truly prosper you will need to change your philosophy about money. I was recently on a plane with my booking agent and we struck up a conversation with two young guys who were seated near us. One of them asked me what I do for a living.

"I'm a speaker," I told him.

"What do you speak about?" he asked me.

"I speak about how to have a millionaire mindset and how to prosper," I replied.

"Money's not important to me," he said.

I looked at him and said, "You're broke, aren't you!"

He replied, "I think things like family and health are much more important than having money."

I knew that he didn't have much money because he had adopted a mindset that says you can have either money or good health and a happy family life, but not both. Why does it have to be an either/or proposition? The answer is, of course, that it doesn't! This young man was stuck in a mindset about money that he had accepted from others and, as is so often the case when it comes to such mindsets, he wasn't even aware of it.

A MILLIONAIRE MINDSET IS NOT ABOUT BREAKING EVEN, IT'S ABOUT BREAKING THROUGH

What's your mindset, my friend? Have you bought into the mindset that is reflected in expressions such as "The rich get richer, the poor get poorer, and the middle class go shopping"? If you tell me your history regarding money, I will be able to describe your current mindset regarding money. I once had a client who was quite a successful businessman, but his goal was always simply to break even. In fact, my nickname for him was 'Mr Break Even'. He had inherited a break even mindset from his father. A millionaire mindset is not about breaking even, it's about breaking through into abundance and profit.

Our outward behaviour will always conform to our internal mindset. That means if we want to change how we act, we first have to change how we think. Dr. Maxwell Maltz, author of the classic self–help book *Psycho Cybernetics,* has said, "Ideas and actions that are contrary to a person's belief system will not be acted and will not be accepted." What this means is that even if you think you want to be wealthy but your life is currently governed by thoughts of lack, then you will never achieve wealth. It's all about how you think. You cannot have two opposing thoughts in one head. For example, you can't think happy and feel sad at the same time (unless you're a woman!).

In order to bring about change in your external world, you have to work on your mind, your attitudes, and the way you think about and construct your life. In your day–to–day life, are you playing offence or defence? Are you waiting for your lucky break or are you busy creating your future? Are you focused on end results or on the process? Are you blaming your past or confronting it? You cannot change what you won't confront. Wrong mindsets that are not confronted take a strong hold over our minds. We become so used to them that we begin to think of them as a natural part of who we are. We begin to say, "That's just the way I think.

It's who I am. I can't change who I am." Yes you can, my friend! You need to change what you constantly tolerate. You need to confront thought patterns and mindsets that keep your prosperity locked up. And you need to be determined to change them.

THE WISE MAN IS THE MASTER OF HIS MIND, BUT THE FOOL IS SLAVE TO HIS MIND

You and I need to be masters of our own minds. As an ancient proverb says, the wise man is the master of his mind, but the fool is slave to his mind. One of my favourite expressions is this: "If it's a mist in here, it's a fog out there." In other words, if we are not clear in our minds, then our whole world will be like a fog around us.

Your mind needs to be like a thermostat rather than a thermometer. A thermometer reacts to the external environment, but a thermostat is proactive and changes the external environment. To change the climate of a room or a building, you set the thermostat and it creates constant climate. In the same way, in order to change your life you have to change your mindset. Rather than simply reacting to the external conditions like a thermometer, your mind needs to control your external conditions like a thermostat.

You and I need to be masters of our own minds.

Your thoughts are like the roots of your life. In order to change the fruits of your life, you first need to change the roots. Be aware of why you think the way you think. Thought patterns can be deep-rooted, so make a decision to become more aware of them and where they came from. There are some thought patterns in our lives that we need to uproot if we are ever to become prosperous.

Statistician W. Edwards Deming, initiator of *Total Quality Management*, found from 50 years of statistical study that if you focus on the first 15 percent of any process and get it right, you will go on to achieve at least 85 percent of your desired outcome. That's why having the right mindset is so important. Developing a millionaire mindset sets you up for great achievement.

CHALLENGE

Before we go any further, think about your mindset right now. What influences in your life — past and present — have shaped the way you think about wealth and prosperity? Are you a 'glass half full' or a 'glass half empty' kind of person? What are your expectations? Is your goal in life just to get by, or to break even? If so, why do you think that way? What thought patterns and mindsets have you been tolerating instead of confronting? Are you ready to confront wrong thinking or will you just 'stay average'?

CHAPTER 4

your thoughts determine your actions

Have you ever looked at a person's clothes and thought, "What were they thinking?" Remember the bell bottom trousers and flares of the Seventies? Mine were so wide it took two days for the front to catch up to the back! When you look at the fashion of the Seventies, you have to wonder what we were thinking! But in reality we didn't really think about it. We just wore what we were told was the fashion of the day and didn't think twice about it. When you see the predicaments that people can get themselves into, it often makes you wonder, "What were they thinking?"

Most wrong thinking is based on wrong information or a wrong premise. If you start with a wrong premise, you will come to a wrong conclusion for all the wrong reasons. For example, if my premise is "people look cool in bell bottom pants", then my conclusion will be that if I put on a pair of bell bottom pants I will look cool. Wrong!

YOUR MINDSET SETS THE COURSE OF YOUR LIFE

Our mindsets set the course of our lives. A mindset is a frame of mind or a pattern of thinking. The millionaire mindset is no different — it's a way of thinking about your potential for wealth and prosperity that creates positive expectation and motivates you to action. Mindsets are formed in the process of interpreting our experiences; things that are said to us, things that are done to us, the way we see people treating each other. If we develop wrong mindsets on the basis of negative experiences, we end up living at a level far beneath where we could and should be living. A wrong mindset can put us on course for disaster. So often people can avoid calamity in their lives simply by changing their thinking.

I remember once speaking at a conference in New Zealand to a group of young Maori people. There was a particular young guy standing at the back of the room who I thought looked really mean. I interpreted his folded arms and tattooed face as an indication that he was a troublesome person, so I became wary of him as I spoke. Imagine my surprise when I later discovered that he was actually a Sunday school teacher! I had started with a wrong premise; that anyone who looked like him must be bad news. I formed a wrong conclusion for all the wrong reasons. That's what prejudice is — prejudging a person or situation before we have all the facts.

I have also been on the receiving end of this kind of prejudice. A friend of mine who was a very successful businessman once gave me a solid gold Rolex Presidential watch as a gift. It was a beautiful watch. It had a diamond face and diamond bezel and was worth about $40,000. At the time, I was involved in running life development programs and events for young people around Australia and abroad, and I was also running rehabilitation programs for young people with life–controlling addictions. I was also involved in working with the poor and underprivileged. I had been quite successful in my work and I was often invited to speak at youth conventions and other such events. I'd also written a number of books that had also been quite successful. By the same token, I was not at that point in my life where I could buy myself a $40,000 Rolex watch!

One day I was signing books at a conference when a very disgruntled gentleman noticed my watch and came up to me with a look of disgust and contempt. He proceeded to tell me that I was a charlatan and a thief. He couldn't fathom that a person who was working among the poor and helping young people with drug addictions and other problems could afford a watch like that. At first I didn't respond. I watched him as he proceeded to tell everybody else around what a charlatan he thought I was.

Later that day, when I stepped up onto the platform to speak, I told the story of how my friend had given me my Rolex watch. The first person at the book table afterwards was my accuser. He apologised to me and told me how sorry he was that he had misjudged me. Without knowing anything about the circumstances of how I had come to own such a nice watch, this man had formulated a wrong premise — that is, that someone who did what I did could only come to own such a watch by dishonest means — and he had therefore come to a wrong conclusion about me.

After he had apologised to me, I took a piece of paper, tore it into little pieces, and threw the pieces of paper into a fan. I said to the man, "I want you to put that piece of paper back together just as it was."

"I can't do that," he said.

"Exactly," I replied. "It can't be done. But that's just what you have done to my name and my credibility. You have formulated a wrong premise and you came to a wrong conclusion about me for all the wrong reasons. You have blackened my name."

We are often too quick to arrive at wrong conclusions based on wrong premises. If you want to be a great thinker, if you want to be a person with a great capacity for wealth and prosperity, if you want to develop a millionaire mindset, then you have got to begin basing your thinking on right premises. The thinking that has brought you to where you are now will not take you to where you want to be.

THE INPUT OF OUR THOUGHTS DETERMINES THE OUTPUT OF OUR ACTIONS

Achieving a millionaire mindset requires a higher level of thinking. Our thoughts determine our lives. The input of our thoughts determines the output of our actions. Here's how it works. It starts with awareness. You need to become aware of how you think and why you think the way you think. Once you've developed this awareness about your thinking, you are in a position to change how you think. If you change your thinking, it will change how you feel; if you change your feelings, it will change how you act; if you change your actions, it will change your level of prosperity. It's a five–stage process:

Awareness → Think → Feel → Act → Live

Sometimes people want to start at the level of feelings. But the key to changing our feelings is to change our thinking first. Here's a practical illustration of how this works. Have you ever been in love? And have you ever felt annoyed with the person you love? Our tendency is to accept our feelings as something we have no control over. "I can't help my feelings," you may say. Yes you can, my friend! You can choose to change your feelings by changing the way you think. Try to think positive thoughts about someone and at the same time continue to feel anger towards them. It's impossible! What we tend to do is to feed our feelings of anger by thinking negative thoughts about the person we are angry with. But if you make a choice to change the way you think, this will change the way you feel about the person, and that in turn will change the way you act towards them. Ultimately, this will change the way you live.

The input of our thoughts determines the output of our actions.

Before we move on, let's consider the whole topic of 'feelings' a little further. One of the greatest traps that people can fall into is the 'feeling' trap — allowing feelings to dictate the circumstances of their lives. Feelings can be very fickle. We need to bring them under the control of correct thinking. Your feelings should be a product of a millionaire mindset that is expressed through your words. They should be a support mechanism to your wealth creation capacity, not a destructive habit that robs you of prosperity.

MANY PEOPLE TEND TO FEEL THEIR WAY RATHER THAN THINK THEIR WAY THROUGH LIFE

Sometimes it seems that the whole world revolves around feelings; so much so that we become virtually enslaved to our feelings. Feelings can be the biggest hindrance to change in our lives. Many people tend to feel their way rather than think their way through life. One of the most common excuses for inaction is "I didn't feel like doing it". So many people live unfulfilled lives because all their action is driven purely by how they feel from one minute to the next. This works in other ways as well. The whole "if it feels good, do it" philosophy is really just another way of saying, "I'm a slave to my feelings." Being driven by negative feelings will never lead us into positive action. We need to make our feelings subject to our thinking so that our actions are ultimately driven not by feelings, but by thought. Once again, if you can change your thinking, you will change your feelings, which in turn will change your actions and therefore your life.

Because of the link between our thoughts and our feelings, we sometimes confuse thinking patterns with feelings. Here are five thinking patterns that people often mistake for feelings:

1. **Enthusiasm.** Enthusiasm is a way of thinking that is all about how you approach things. Someone once said that an enthusiast is someone who is perfectly sure of the things about which he is mistaken. Henry Ford, founder of the Ford Motor Company, once said, "Enthusiasm is at the bottom of all progress. With it there is accomplishment. Without it there are only alibis." We need an enthusiastic mindset so that we always approach situations and opportunities with positive expectation. An enthusiastic mindset will translate into feelings of optimism.

2. **Attitude.** Attitude is a way of thinking that is all about how we view things. In the Bible story of David and Goliath, the Israelite army had a perception that Goliath was too big to hit. But David's perception of the situation was that Goliath was too big to miss! Attitude is all about mindset. Having a positive attitude puts us in a position to recognise and maximise every opportunity. As the American financier and presidential advisor Bernard Baruch said, "You can become anything if you don't belly ache." Winston Churchill once said, "A pessimist sees a difficulty in every opportunity; an optimist sees the opportunity in every difficulty."

3. **Happiness.** Many people think happiness is a feeling, but it is quite possible to be happy without necessarily feeling happy.

Happiness is actually all about contentment, and contentment is a mindset, not a feeling. You cannot be discontented and be happy. Abraham Lincoln said this: "Most folks are as happy as they make up their minds to be." Or as Martha Washington, wife of George Washington, observed, "I have learnt from experience that the greater part of our happiness or misery depends on our dispositions and not on our circumstances."

4. **Depression.** Depression is a state of mind, not an emotional state. At one time in my life, I suffered from depression for over 18 months. Then one day I had what could almost be described as an awakening; I started to think, "I don't want to be depressed anymore!" As a result of this change of mindset, I managed to throw off my depression. Depression results from a thought pattern that is all about hopelessness and gloom. To get rid of depression you need to change the way you think.

I recently read a disturbing newspaper article about the increasing incidence of Attention Deficit Hyperactivity Disorder (ADHD) among children in countries such as Australia, Canada and the USA. The article reported that powerful cocktails of psychotropic drugs such as Ritalin are being prescribed for children as young as four years old, and in some cases the prescriptions are in adult doses. Some children are being given a range of medications for a range of apparent disorders in addition to ADHD, such as anxiety and depression. Needless to say, controversy is raging around this practice. Teachers have described children on large doses of medication sitting in class in a zombie–like state. Instead of medicating the magic out of our kids just because we don't like the way they behave, we'd do better by trying to understand the underlying causes of their behavioural problems. You can't medicate thoughts that come from a broken heart; in situations like that you need to deal with the root causes before the resultant behaviour will change.

5. **Confidence.** When sports people are interviewed just prior to participating in high–level competition, we often hear interviewers ask questions like, "How confident are you feeling?" The truth is, confidence is a mindset, not a feeling. Confidence is a way of thinking based on your level of preparation. When you are well prepared you are confident. You might feel nervous, but you are confident in the knowledge that you have prepared for the challenge you are about to face.

I have said that our actions are ultimately determined by our thoughts or mindsets. At the same time, however, behaviour can also influence our thought life. One of the behaviours that can often undermine our thought patterns is our speech. Usually, our words express our thoughts. But the words we speak can also have a significant influence on our mindsets. We need to pay close attention to the things we say and the words we allow to dominate important areas of our lives, such as our relationships, our financial world, and our physical wellbeing.

DEATH AND LIFE ARE IN THE POWER OF THE TONGUE

Words have the power to create or destroy us. There's an ancient proverb that says, "Death and life are in the power of the tongue." Consider the following quotation from the Bible:

We all make many mistakes, but those who control their tongues can also control themselves in every other way. We can make a large horse turn around and go wherever we want by means of a small bit in its mouth. And a tiny rudder makes a huge ship turn wherever the pilot wants it to go, even though the winds are strong. So also, the tongue is a small thing, but what enormous damage it can do. A tiny spark can set a great forest on fire. And the tongue is a flame of fire. It...can ruin your whole life. It can turn the entire course of your life into a blazing flame of destruction...[2]

Words can be incredibly destructive. Wars have been started over nothing more than a few words. Words can destroy marriages and friendships. Words can also destroy human potential. Think about a time

[2] James 3:2–6 (New Living Translation)

in your life where you have felt devastated by someone else's words; the time as a small child you ran crying to your parents because one of your buddies told you that you weren't his friend anymore; the time the teacher told you you'd never amount to anything; the time someone criticised your work or told you that you weren't very good at something that you loved doing. Consider what impact those words have had on your life.

On the other hand, words also have the capacity to create. Think of some of the great speeches of history: Abraham Lincoln's Gettysburg Address, Martin Luther King Jr's "I have a dream...", Winston Churchill's "We shall never surrender...". Such words have inspired whole nations and changed the course of history. People will pay hundreds of dollars to listen to great motivational speakers or to read their writings because of the great impact of their words on people's lives. (Hopefully, you're having that kind of experience right now!) Think about a time in which you felt like you were on top of the world simply because someone said to you something as simple as, "Well done!" Think about a time when someone else's words have inspired you to achieve something that you wouldn't otherwise have attempted. Think about the influence words have had on your life.

The good news is that if you know how to speak, then all the power of words is at your disposal. It's right there on the tip of your tongue — literally! One of the best ways to change the way we think about something is to start speaking differently. When we speak positively about our lives, we reinforce positive mindsets and therefore generate positive feelings, which in turn lead to positive actions that have a positive impact on our lives. Our words then become a self–fulfilling prophecy.

CHALLENGE

You can start building a millionaire mindset today simply by starting to speak positively about yourself and your world. If negative words have brought you down or held you back in the past, then you can change that today by neutralising the power of those words. If someone has told you you're no good, start declaring to yourself what a great person you are. If you've been told that your task is impossible or that you'll never make it, start telling yourself that you are going to make it, that it can be done and you are going to do it. If you've been told that you're just average, start telling yourself that you are outstanding, that you are way above average. If there are things in your world that you want to see change, start talking about those things as though they are changing.

If both death and life are in the power of the tongue, then it's up to you to make the choice. My advice to you is to choose life!

If there are things in your world that you want to see change, start talking about those things as though they are changing.

CHAPTER 5

change your mind

Developing a millionaire mindset means increasing the capacity of your thinking. As William Arthur Ward once said, "Nothing limits achievement like small thinking, and nothing expands possibilities like unleashed thinking." The only limitations on our minds are the ones we put on ourselves.

We really need to be vigilant in not allowing other people to project wrong thoughts and mindsets onto us. People often take on another person's thinking patterns and mindsets without ever really considering whether the mindsets they are adopting are constructive. For example, a person experiencing a marriage crisis may go to a friend for advice, but there may be a problem if that friend has had three failed marriages herself! Her thinking and mindset about marriage may not be the most helpful!

Long–term mindsets develop as a result of the way in which we respond to individual experiences and situations. The experience itself is not the real issue. What really matters is how we respond. Two people can have very similar experiences but respond very differently and, as a result, they each develop very different mindsets. For example, two people might go out, get drunk, and later regret what they've done. So, they both have a similar experience. One of them responds by deciding never to get drunk again. He declares, "What a waste! How could I have done that to myself? I am better than that." The other person thinks to himself, "Looks like I am never going to be able to break this cycle." The first person's response develops an overcoming mindset that puts him in charge of his life. The second person's response develops a defeatist mindset that makes him a slave to habit. How you perceive your experiences and respond to your experiences will determine how you live in the long run.

There is a story of two shoe salesmen who go to Africa. One of them quickly writes back to his employer, "Please send me a ticket home. I have no hope of selling shoes here because nobody here wears shoes." The other salesman also writes home: "Please send me a thousand pairs of shoes as soon as you can. There is a great opportunity for us because nobody here wears shoes!" Same experience, different responses. Why? Because they think differently. They have different mindsets.

In Australia we have what we call the 'tall poppy syndrome'. People with a tall poppy syndrome are always cutting successful people down to size in an attempt to bring them down to a common level of mediocrity. Tall poppy syndrome is really just a euphemism for a poverty mindset. People with a poverty mindset hate the idea that others may be more successful than they are. Instead of looking for mentors, all they want to do is tear down people who have achieved wealth and prosperity. On the other hand, a millionaire mindset makes wealthy people mentors, not villains.

HOW DO YOU CHANGE THE WAY YOU THINK?

The big question is, of course, how do I go about changing the way I think? One strategy you can adopt is a therapeutic technique called the 'miracle question'. It goes like this:

> Imagine when you go to bed tonight that while you are asleep a miracle happens. The effect of this miracle is that the problems that brought you to read this book are resolved, but you don't know this because you are still asleep. When you awake tomorrow morning, what will be the first thing you notice that will tell you that this problem has been resolved?

The idea of this technique is to help you to begin thinking differently about your life and to begin to imagine what your world could be like. The simple solution is to start thinking and acting as though things have changed today. Again, it's like the thermometer/thermostat analogy — instead of your thoughts and actions reacting to your external environment like a thermometer, set your mental thermostat so that it changes your external environment.

> *How you perceive your experiences and respond to your experiences will determine how you live in the long run.*

My friend, your actions are determined by your thought patterns. When you think a certain way, you will act accordingly. Often we are not conscious of how our thinking determines our behaviour because we have developed patterns of thought that have become habitual. We need to begin to recognise thought habits that are non–productive, ineffective, dysfunctional or wrong, and begin to change our thinking. When someone is in a bad mood, we often describe it by saying, "They got up on the wrong side of the bed!" We say this as if all it takes to change a bad mood is to swap which side of the bed we sleep on. A person who is in a bad mood is often someone who has succumbed to a habit of thinking that has affected that person in a negative way. That person needs to become aware of their mood and make a decision to change their mindset.

CHALLENGE

There are a number of things you can do to develop a millionaire mindset. Here are four basic strategies:

1. **RENEW** your mind. The cells in your body are being renewed every day. Our body gets rid of old cells and is always replacing them with new ones. We need to do the same with our minds. We need to be proactive in depositing new positive thoughts into our minds every day.

2. **REPLACE** old mindsets. When something you own is no longer serving you well, what do you do? You get a new one! It's the same with mindsets. If the mindset you have today is

not going to get you to where you want to go in life, get a new one. Trade in your old mindset for a millionaire mindset. Even the most positive thoughts we have will be short–lived if we hold on to negative mindsets. If we don't actually change our old thinking habits or patterns, then the positive thought will soon be overpowered. We have to consciously get rid of old mindsets, then start to replace them with new patterns of thinking.

For example, if your mindset about marriage is that marriage is a drag, then even the best marriage seminar in the world that presents marriage in a wonderful positive light isn't going to be enough to change you. You actually need to stop thinking of marriage as a drag and develop a mindset that says, "Marriage is great! I love being married! I love the person I'm married to!" It's about putting in the effort required to replace old mindsets with new ones.

Begin seeing the world around you as being full of opportunity rather than impossibility.

3. **REALIGN** your thinking by regularly asking yourself, "Is this the right way to think?" Become a little introspective. Think about your thinking. When you find yourself acting in a way that is not conducive to increasing your prosperity, ask yourself, "Why am I acting like this? What's going on in my head right now? What mindset is causing me to behave in this way? How should I be thinking? What needs to change in my head?"

4. **RE–ESTABLISH** your convictions. Some things in life are a matter of preference, but others are a matter of conviction. A preference is usually something we can take up or leave behind. I might prefer chocolate ice cream to vanilla, but if there's no chocolate left I'm not going to lose any sleep over it. I'm going to say, "What the heck, vanilla will be fine." But when something is a matter of conviction, it becomes non–negotiable. A conviction is not a thought you possess, it is a thought that

possesses you. Convictions are the things that people are prepared to make great sacrifices for. Some people even die for their convictions. What convictions drive your life? Are your convictions propelling you forward into a life of success and wealth? Is prosperity a preference for you or a conviction? Is prosperity non–negotiable in your life?

Make up your mind today to change your mind. Start thinking bigger. Expand your capacity. Don't let all those bare feet put you off selling more shoes! Begin seeing the world around you as being full of opportunity rather than impossibility. That's a millionaire mindset!

CHAPTER 6

overcome negative mindsets

Negative mindsets can come from a wide range of sources. Perhaps at some time in your life someone has labelled you a 'failure', a 'loser', a 'no–hoper', or an 'underachiever'. Labels such as these can create negative mindsets about ourselves. We need to reject such labels and not allow them to gain power over our minds.

Have you ever had a teacher say to you statements like: "You'll never amount to much!", "You don't have what it takes!", and "You'll always be an average achiever!"? Statements such as these can have a powerful influence on the way you think about yourself. You need to refuse to accept statements like these.

Another source of negative mindsets can be our upbringing. Parents and family are typically our earliest role models and we can tend to take on their worldviews without even realising it. What kind of upbringing did you have? Were you encouraged to think big and dream big? Or were you taught not to expect much from life? Were you encouraged to stand out from the crowd and believe in yourself? Or were you told not to make a fuss and just try to blend in with the crowd? Did your upbringing provide you with positive role models for your relationships? Or were all your relationship models dysfunctional? We need to be able to identify any negative mindsets that may have set in during our upbringing. We need to understand where they came from so that we can deal with them. Your greatest war is fought in your mind; it's where the greatest battles are won and lost.

OUR MINDSETS INFLUENCE OUR PERCEPTION OF REALITY

My two daughters have been brought up with a prosperity mindset. Other people are brought up without a prosperity mentality. Interestingly, two people can have very similar upbringings but develop very different mindsets. I know of two brothers who have developed two very different mindsets, despite the same upbringing. One grew up thinking his father was a tightwad, while the other never thought of his father as anything but generous. In actual fact, he treated them both the same. But because they each had a different mindset about their father, they had different perceptions of his behaviour toward them. One reality, but two different mindsets resulted in different perceptions of that reality. Your mindset has a powerful influence over how you perceive and experience reality.

In my own life, I have no recollection of my father ever denying me anything. I never had a problem asking him for anything. Some people grow up with strong controlling personalities and develop a fear of asking for things. They feel nervous going to the boss to ask for a raise. I've learnt to be a 'master asker'. I'm not afraid to ask.

To have a millionaire mindset, you need to become a 'master asker'. That means you need to know:

- **When to ask.** Timing is important. There's a right time to ask and a wrong time to ask. Wait till all the circumstances are most favourable, then ask.

- **What to ask for.** Know exactly what it is you want. Don't ask for one thing when what you really need is something else. For example, don't ask for advice when what you really need is information; don't ask for a loan when what you really need is a donation; don't ask for a minute of your time when you really need a couple of hours. Be accurate in what you ask for and be specific.

- **How to ask.** Learn the art of persuasion. Think about the best way to approach the person you want something from and be diplomatic. I'm not talking about manipulation, flattery or deceit. It's a matter of using some common sense and wisdom and knowing the best way to go about asking in order to get a positive response.

- **Who to ask.** Don't ask just anybody. If you need advice in investing, you won't ask your motor mechanic. If your car needs fixing, you won't take it to your dentist. If you need money, don't ask someone who doesn't have any. Figure out exactly what you need, then decide whom the best person would be to ask for help.

- **Why that person will want to give you what you need.** Before you ask, make sure you know why it is in that person's interests to give you what you're asking for. Know the answer to the question, "Why should I help you?" Make sure you understand what's in it for them.

As children, many of us asked for things and were told, "No, we can't afford that! Do you think money grows on trees? Do you think we're made of money?" Constantly hearing these answers creates a blueprint for your life. From then on, your expectation is that if you ask for anything, the answer will always be "No!" From then on, every time you want to ask for something, you may stop and think, "So what's the point of asking?"

The millionaire mindset plays mental golf — always moving forward, aiming for a specific point up ahead, trying to take the most direct path possible.

We need to create a positive environment around our minds. Things thrive in the environment to which they are suited. To be prosperous, you need to create an environment that supports prosperity. If you have negative mindsets about things like wealth, prosperity and success, you need to be coached and trained to change your way of thinking.

Sometimes we are brought up a certain way and we become committed to staying there because we're worried about what everyone else thinks. The truth is, other people don't think about you that often! I was once doing some individual coaching with a client who was one of the top real estate agents in New Zealand. She said to me, "Pat, I know I could get to another level if I just stopped worrying about what other people think of me."

I said to her, "You know, they don't think of you that often." And it was like a light went on in her head.

I then said, "You play ping–pong in your head all day. 'What will they think?' 'What should I do?' In fact, I predict that right now you are in a state of indecision."

"How do you know that?" she asked, astonished. "You're right. This morning at home I was discussing with my husband whether or not to go to a party tonight. I really want to go and he wants to go, but we're so worried about these other people being there and how we're going to have a terrible time…"

I interrupted her, "Why are you allowing someone else to dictate to you about whether or not you have fun and do what you want to do? Make a decision and stick to it."

"Okay, we're going to the party," she replied.

"And you're going to have a good time," I told her.

"We're going to have a damn good time!" she stated defiantly.

She rang her husband right away and told him they were going to the party. She stopped playing mental ping–pong.

EN ROUTE TO SUCCESS, THE GROUND IS USUALLY FULL OF UPS AND DOWNS

The millionaire mindset doesn't play mental ping–pong, repeatedly tossing a decision back and forward and never actually making any progress. If anything, the millionaire mindset plays mental golf — always moving forward, aiming for a specific point up ahead, trying to take the most direct path possible. Of course, the most direct path is rarely the path you will take. En route to success, the ground is usually not flat but full of ups and downs; there are usually one or two rough patches you have to find your way out of; there are always a few traps to be avoided; and occasionally you might find the water and have to play your shot again. But while your shots might not always go according to plan, no matter what happens, you always continue to move forward with your end point in mind (even if it's not always in sight!).

You've got to make up your mind to shift your thinking. You've got to get your thinking to another level.

Another obstacle that preserves negative mindsets in our lives is excuses. Excuses are the means by which we attempt to justify our shortcomings. Excuses are ammunition we use against ourselves in acts of self–sabotage. Blame is a type of excuse. Some people are constantly looking for reasons why things are not working for them, so they blame it on their lack of progress and prosperity. They blame the market, they blame the product, they blame their colleagues, and they blame the boss. Sometimes they blame things like their past or their upbringing. Ultimately, these are no more than paltry excuses that people use to justify a lack of vision and a lack of capacity for increase. The truth is, it's your choice. You can choose excuses or a millionaire mindset — you can't have both.

STOP USING EXCUSES AND START FINDING REASONS WHY YOU CAN MOVE AHEAD

People make excuses for all sorts of things. Some people make excuses for being overweight. They say things like, "I've had five children" or "I was big as a child." Others make excuses based on their past. They might say, "I was brought up in a dysfunctional home." Still others use lack of knowledge as an excuse. These people say, "I was never taught that." At the end of the day, my response to all such excuses is, "So what?" The moment you seek to excuse yourself, you sabotage your advancement. Everyone has stuff they have to deal with. So what's the big deal? It's not like we've all taken a pain inoculation pill. Instead of using excuses for our lack of advancement, we need to ask ourselves the question, "What am I going to do about it?" Stop using excuses and start finding reasons why you *can* move ahead.

Recently, a woman in one of my mentoring groups said to me, "I am always late for work."

"Why are you always late?" I asked.

"I don't really know. I always try to get to work on time," she said.

"That's your problem," I told her. "You are trying to get to work on time so you get up at a certain hour, but most things generally take more time than you allow. Here is what you need to do: don't try to get to work *on time;* try to get there *early.* You may just arrive on time."

She was looking for an excuse for being late; I helped her find a reason she could arrive on time.

Tennis great Virginia Wade played at Wimbledon for 15 years straight without ever winning the title. Several other wins at the US Open and the Australian Open were not able to fill the gap left by so many winless Wimbledons. Wade had got caught up in making excuses — bad luck, bad weather, poor line calls, bad bounces — she found all kinds of excuses to explain her failure to win a Wimbledon title. Then, in 1977, Virginia Wade adopted a more proactive approach to her tennis. She gave up making excuses and committed herself to winning at Wimbledon. No matter what circumstances were in front of her, she refused to make any more excuses. She took personal responsibility for her own mistakes and the quality of her game and her competitive spirit (or lack thereof). In 1977, Virginia Wade won her first Wimbledon championship.

NOBODY IS A REAL LOSER UNTIL THEY START BLAMING SOMEBODY ELSE

John Wooden was one of the greatest basketball coaches of all time. He led his team, the UCLA Bruins, to a record–breaking number of NCAA basketball championships and gained the respect of players and spectators alike. He was inspirational — he led and propelled his teams to many great victories. He always admonished his players to take responsibility for their actions. One of his memorable motivating statements was this: "Nobody is a real loser until they start blaming somebody else."

Are you in the habit of making excuses? If you are, stop it! You were designed for advancement, you were engineered for prosperity, and you have been endowed with seeds of greatness. Excuses short circuit your destiny and create the opposite kind of life to the one you are meant to have. Broke people make excuses; people with a millionaire mindset make a life. No more excuses!

With prosperity comes a certain amount of responsibility that cannot be excused. The ability to accept responsibility is the measure of a person. The ability to accept responsibility for your own prosperity is the measure of how much prosperity will come to you. Unfortunately, some people recognise responsibility only to avoid it. They are always busy doing something other than what they should be doing because it is easier and allows them to avoid responsibility. The millionaire mindset, however, doesn't dodge responsibility. It faces it head on and acts upon it. Responsibility creates within us a capacity for greater wealth and prosperity.

One final negative mindset I want to address is this: some people think that you have to be educated to be able to become wealthy. This is just not true! Education does not equal wealth. I have met countless highly educated people who are unable to live successful and prosperous lives. At the same time, all over the world there are high school drop-outs who have been very successful people like Bill Gates, Thomas Edison, Federico Fellini and Steve Jobs. William Feather, author of *The Business of Life*, made this remark: "Two delusions fostered by higher education are that what is taught corresponds to what is learned, and that it will somehow pay off in money." Mark Twain put it aptly when he said, "I never let my schooling interfere with my education." Remember, you do not have to be educated, you just have to think with a millionaire mindset.

CHALLENGE

Here is a great remedy for excuses: develop positive expectations. Expect things to go well, expect yourself to prosper, expect to be wealthy, expect to be on time, expect to lose weight, expect to be healthy, and expect to develop great friendships. Expectation is the breeding ground for miracles.

My friend, I have found that whatever we focus our attention on will grow. If you focus your attention on making excuses, then your excuses will flourish; if you focus on creating wealth, then that will expand. If you spend your mental energy on constantly worrying, excusing and justifying, it will be difficult, if not impossible, to create abundance in your life.

So determine to focus on your success, expect wealth, get rid of all excuses from your life, and begin to see great results!

CHAPTER 7

how do you see yourself: as a pauper or prosperous?

A critical factor in developing a millionaire mindset is to develop a healthy view of yourself. How do you see yourself? Do you see yourself as a person who deserves to prosper? Do you see yourself as a person who has the potential and the ability to become prosperous? Or do you feel 'unworthy' of prosperity? Perhaps you think that prosperity is beyond you, that you 'don't have what it takes'. Sterling W. Sill said this: "Wealth is not only what you have, but it is also what you are."

The reason many people don't prosper is not because of their lack of ability or their circumstances, but rather because of who they are, or more precisely, who they think or feel they are and how they see themselves. The level of prosperity in your life will be determined to a large extent by who you are as a person.

To be prosperous, you need to have a clear picture of the person you believe you can be. You will naturally gravitate towards the dominant image of yourself in your mind. If thoughts of anxiety are your dominant mindset, then you'll gravitate towards anxiety. It's like trying to hit a dartboard with a dart when you're facing another direction. To hit a target you must be facing the direction of the target and focusing on the target.

THE BIGGEST HINDRANCE TO PROSPERITY IS A WRONG MINDSET

Many people get into a rut in their thinking. When they think about themselves, they don't believe they deserve to prosper. They think that increase will never happen. Remember, the only difference between a rut and a grave is time! Don't die with prosperity still in you! You need to learn to think like this: Who deserves nice things? You do! Who deserves a prosperous family? You do! Who deserves a nice home? You do! Who deserves to wear nice clothes? You do! Who deserves to have a life that is advancing with wealth and increase? You do! You deserve these things! The biggest hindrance to prosperity is not a lack of money, it's a wrong mindset. Change how you see yourself and others. Your life will not be able to advance until your mind is set to advance. Your view of wealth is wealth's view of you.

When you look at yourself, what do you see? What images of you dominate your life? Whatever images you have of yourself are what you will actually gravitate towards — they become self–fulfilling prophecies. You cannot have two competing thoughts at the same time — one thought will always dominate. If you are thinking you'd love to be more prosperous but your dominant mentality about yourself is "I'm not worth much", then you will never be prosperous.

UNTIL YOU SEE YOURSELF AS PROSPEROUS, PROSPERITY WILL ELUDE YOU

If you are reading this book and thinking, "I really would like to be prosperous, but I don't believe I have the effort, energy and focus needed to become a prosperous person", then you have two competing thoughts in your mind and at some point one of them will overcome the other. If on the one hand you desire prosperity, and yet on the other hand your mindset is one of lack (not enough, not good enough, not doing enough), then this negative mindset will dominate your self–image. Until you begin to see yourself as a person who has the capacity to be prosperous, prosperity will continue to elude you.

Perspective is so important to prosperity. The way we respond to life's many challenges forms imprints in our minds called perspectives. Life impacts us all in so many different ways that each of us has developed our own unique perspectives. For example, when you stand on top of a mountain, the direction you face determines your perspective. Where you stand determines what you see. When you face north, you get a northern perspective. When you face south, you get a southern perspective. We see many different perspectives even on the same mountain.

I've known people who have been involved in identical businesses, and yet one has succeeded while the other one has failed! The bottom line is this: the underlying difference is their perspective.

The way we respond to life's many challenges forms imprints in our minds called perspectives.

DEVELOP A FREER ATTITUDE ABOUT PROSPERITY

How do you see yourself? I once bought a beautiful silk tie that was quite expensive. When I told a friend how much it had cost me, he was absolutely shocked that I would spend so much on a tie. But to me that is not extravagant. In my role as a public speaker, I want to look good and feel good about myself. I cannot stand in front of people and challenge them to develop the mindset of a millionaire if I'm not practising what I preach. I dress according to the image that I want to project. I dress according to what I think I am worth. I perceive value in myself. Rather than thinking, "That's too much to pay for a tie", I prefer to think, "I deserve to wear a tie like that. I'm worth it!" It's not about being conceited or arrogant or narcissistic; it's about valuing yourself and developing freer attitudes about money, wealth and prosperity.

Until you learn to value yourself properly, you will not be able to develop a millionaire mindset. Why? Because you will lack the motivation needed to pursue a life of true prosperity. "But..." I hear you ask, "Isn't it really more important to value other people? Shouldn't my motivation to be wealthy stem from a desire to help others?" My answer is, "Yes!" But it is not possible to value other people any more than you value yourself. One of the great principles of the Christian faith is the requirement to "love your neighbour *as yourself*". This implies that you can only love your neighbour if you first love yourself. A millionaire mindset places a high value on self, and then turns that outward by placing equally high value on other people.

To illustrate, let me tell you a bit about myself. When I was a kid, my family didn't have much. I wanted desperately to earn some money. So at the age of 10 I went and got my first job. Now, the Sydney suburb of Bankstown is not the greatest thriving metropolis in the world. It's a very multicultural area of Sydney. It had a lot of economic problems, but it was a community to which a lot of Lebanese, Greeks and Italians migrated. My own family migrated there from Italy. In fact, at school we used to play a game called 'Spot the Aussie'.

I got my first job at a fruit and vegetable market in Bankstown. I remember I used to earn 40 cents an hour packing potatoes into plastic bags. I became so good at packing potatoes that I was soon promoted to packing onions as well. You see, I discovered that I could do two things at once – unlike most men!

REWARD IS A GREAT MOTIVATOR

Across the road was another fruit and vegetable shop owned by an Italian man by the name of Peter. Peter had heard of my skills as a potato packer and then as an onion packer. My fame had spread throughout the Bankstown fruit market community. There I was, the spud packer champion of Bankstown. (I may be short, but I've got very fast hands.) Peter began to headhunt me. Instead of offering me 40 cents an hour, he told me he would give me 10 cents a bag. I immediately realised that my value was increasing. My perspective began to change. I began to see myself as the fastest spud packer in Bankstown because I was now paid by the bag, not by the hour. My perspective changed as my productivity increased. Reward is a great motivator. My productivity increased because my value increased.

Years later, as a high school student I wanted to buy a guitar, so my Dad got me a job at Victa Lawn Mowers. I worked on the assembly line and I was paid about three to four dollars an hour. Years later I took on a position working with youth in a local church. I was paid the huge sum of $140 a week! I realized that I would have to supplement my income, so I went back to the fruit market – this time it was the Flemington Fruit Market. I didn't realize how much the fame of my childhood exploits had spread throughout the fruit market community, but when I walked in on the first day of my job people stared at me in absolute awe. They began to say, "It's him! He's no taller than he was, but he looks older!" They asked me, "Is it you?"

"Yes, it is I," I replied. "It is Pat Mesiti, the fastest spud packer in Bankstown!"

So I went to work every day, starting at four o'clock in the morning and working until 10am to supplement my income. Now, fast forward to 2005. I recently flew to Europe to speak and I was paid $10,000 an hour. What's changed? I'm the same person, same height, same name, and same looks. What has changed is my value to the market place.

The other week I was offered a huge sum of money to do some work for a company. My first reaction was: why would they call me? Then it dawned on me: of course they would call me! Who else would they call? You see, it's the value I bring to people and to organisations that quantifies what I earn.

NET WORTH IS RELATED TO SELF WORTH

Your net worth is directly related to your self worth. If you work on your self, your value will grow. Many people think they are paid for their time, but they're not – they're paid for their value.

People have tried to stick a mind virus in me, telling me, "You can't make that much money! You're just a Bankstown boy! You'll always be a Bankstown boy. You can take the boy out of Bankstown, but you can't take Bankstown out of the boy." Well, I really believe you can. You can change if you choose to. It really starts with your mindset and you've got to start today.

CHALLENGE

Ask yourself this question: "Do I really value myself?" What value do you place on your mind and your knowledge? Do you baulk at the cost of attending a seminar that might help you improve your mind? If you truly value yourself, you won't think twice about spending money on self–improvement. A negative mindset will say, "That's a luxury I can't justify!" A positive and healthy mindset will say, "I am worth it!" To develop a millionaire mindset, you need to see yourself in a new light. If you've always thought of yourself as a pauper, start seeing yourself as a prince. If you don't value yourself as much as you should, then start to speak differently about yourself and act differently towards yourself. Go and buy yourself a nice tie or a new dress. Tell yourself that you deserve it, that you are worth it.

CHAPTER 8

the millionaire mindset

So far I have talked a lot about a millionaire mindset and some of the adjustments we need to make in our lives in order to develop a millionaire mindset. In this chapter I want to look a little more closely at what kind of thinking makes up a millionaire mindset. In other words, what is 'prosperity thinking'? How does a wealthy person think? For a start, as we've already discovered, people with a millionaire mindset think bigger than others around them. They don't think, "I can't afford a top shelf donut." They live out of a mindset of unlimited possibility.

Here are a few characteristics of a millionaire mindset. This list is not exhaustive, but it will help you begin to understand what kind of thinking it takes to become a candidate for a life of continually increasing prosperity.

CHARACTERISTIC #1

Having a millionaire mindset means you play to win as opposed to simply playing not to lose. At half time in the 2005 soccer final of the European Champions League, AC Milan had a 3–0 lead over Liverpool. Then, in the second half, Liverpool scored three goals in six minutes and went on to win the final in a penalty shoot–out. AC Milan went from playing to win to playing to defend their 3–0 lead and ended up losing the match. A person with a millionaire mindset always stays on the front foot pushing forward, no matter how far in front they might be. A millionaire mindset plays to advance and to win, not merely to maintain a level or a lead.

CHARACTERISTIC #2

A person with a millionaire mindset is a person who is constantly asking questions and finding answers. Unlike the person with a poverty mindset, they don't assume that they already know it all. They are inquisitive, not constantly opinionated. Rather than being an armchair expert, a prosperity thinker is always learning something new. When they are in conversation with someone who knows more than they do about some area, they don't try to pretend that they know more than they do. Instead, they adopt a learning attitude and defer to the superior knowledge of the other person. They see it as an opportunity to expand their own understanding. In fact, with a millionaire mindset, every new meeting is treated not as an opportunity to show the other person how much he knows, but as an opportunity to learn something new from the other person.

> *Rather than being an armchair expert, a prosperity thinker is always learning something new.*

CHARACTERISTIC #3

The millionaire mindset is able to ignore criticism. I don't listen to my critics; I listen to my mentors and leaders, the people I have given permission to speak into my life. Donald Trump says that he doesn't listen to everybody, only to his 'somebodies'. Successful people tend to be criticised more than anyone else, so to be successful you need to be able to ignore your critics. Criticism usually comes from people who have a poverty mindset. They develop stereotypes of wealthy people and immediately assume that if you are wealthy you must be no good. They say, "I wonder how many people he had to walk over to get to where he is?" or "I bet she has never done a hard day's work in her life!" People who say things like this are really expressing a mindset of lack. Because they don't think of themselves as having the potential to prosper, they resent people who have achieved prosperity.

CHARACTERISTIC #4

A person with a millionaire mindset goes beyond desire to commitment. It's not enough just to want to be prosperous — you have to be passionately committed to becoming prosperous. Life follows our convictions and our focus, not our desires. Desire is a starting point, but as long as something remains only in the realm of desire, it is only an option. When I was head of a drug rehabilitation organization, there were young men who desired to break their addiction, but unless they were prepared to focus on changing and being totally committed to changing, their desire was not enough to get them there. When we move from the realm of desire to the realm of commitment, that which was optional becomes non–negotiable.

Life follows our convictions and our focus, not our desires.

CHARACTERISTIC #5

People with a millionaire mindset have a different understanding of their personal worth. They develop their self worth before they develop their net worth. You can be paid either for your time or for the value you bring to people. A poverty mindset sees time as the primary basis for payment — you work a certain number of hours and get paid on an hourly basis. This means that your level of prosperity is determined by your hourly rate and the amount of time you are able to give to your work. A person with a millionaire mindset understands that time is irrelevant to prosperity and that wealth is much more about who they are and what they do than it is about how many hours they work.

CHARACTERISTIC #6

To have a millionaire mindset is to recognise the need for mentors, people you can look up to and from whom you can seek guidance and inspiration. These are people who have been successful and achieved things that you are still aiming to achieve.

CHARACTERISTIC #7

Millionaire mindset people use what is in their hand to do what's in their heart. People with a poverty mindset are not driven by what's in their heart and, as a result, their hands are tied. People like Sir Bob Geldof and U2 lead singer Bono are passionate about causes such as the elimination of poverty in the world. They have used their celebrity status as rock stars to try to influence world leaders to bring about change, as was evidenced by the recent 'Live 8' global rock concert. "Celebrity is ridiculous," Bono says. "It's silly, but it's a kind of currency, and you have to spend it wisely." He is using what's in his hand to do what's in his heart. Start by asking yourself what's in your heart. What's your dream? What's your passion? Now ask yourself this: "What do I have in my hand today that I can utilise to start moving in the direction of what's in my heart?" That's a millionaire mindset.

CHARACTERISTIC #8

A person with a millionaire mindset uses money to buy outcomes and memories, not just material possessions. A person with a poverty mindset uses money simply to buy 'things'. Have you ever heard someone say something like this: "Why would anyone want to spend $5,000 on a five–day holiday? Once it's over, you've got nothing to show for it. If I had $5,000 I'd buy a new plasma television!" This reflects a poverty mindset that sees money purely as something to be used to buy stuff.

I remember being in a poor area of a large city in the UK once when I noticed that despite the poverty of the community, every house had a television satellite dish on the roof. A prosperity mindset is less utilitarian and sees money as a key to an enriched life. Instead of simply spending money on 'stuff', a prosperous person spends money to enhance relationships, to have new experiences, to buy memories, and to make life better for other people.

CHARACTERISTIC #9

A millionaire mindset recognises the importance of seed, whereas a person with a poverty mindset is concerned only with the fruit. Everything in life starts as a seed. Something that might look small and insignificant today could be the seed of something that will change the world tomorrow. Napoleon Hill, author of the seminal book *Think and Grow Rich*, once said, "The world is full of unfortunate souls who didn't hear opportunity knock at the door because they were down at the convenience store buying lottery tickets." Such people are trying to generate fruit in their lives without an understanding that fruit is the end result of a process that begins with the planting of a seed. As a result, when a seed of opportunity presents itself, they fail to see the potential in it.

A millionaire mindset is looking for acorns, not oak trees.

A person with a millionaire mindset lives with an awareness that every day of our lives could be a day of opportunity, a day where there is a seed to be seized and planted. Sometimes the seed is easily missed because seeds by nature are very small. The giant oak tree grows from a tiny acorn. All the potential greatness of the oak tree lies in that acorn. If the acorn is never planted, the tree will never grow. A millionaire mindset is looking for acorns, not oak trees. Is your focus on the size of the tree or on the seed from which the tree grows?

CHARACTERISTIC #10

Another important characteristic of the millionaire mindset is the quality of courage. In his book, *The Millionaire Mind*, Thomas J. Stanley identifies courage to take financial risks as something most self–made millionaires have in common. Now, Stanley argues that taking risks does not mean gambling. In fact, very few millionaires gamble at all. Here are a few millionaire mindset principles about courage and risk–taking that were revealed by a group of millionaires whom Stanley surveyed: [3]

- Think of success, not failure. In taking risks, understand what the probable outcomes will be. Then do whatever you can to improve the chance of getting the outcome you desire.
- Believe in yourself and be prepared to work hard. These are two ways of reducing fear and anxiety and bolstering your courage.
- To build belief in yourself, prepare and plan for success, focus on the key issues, and be well organised.
- Playing competitive sports is a good way to develop the mental toughness needed to handle fear. Develop the attitude and discipline of a successful sportsperson. Develop both physical and mental strength and courage.
- Strong religious faith is an important factor for almost 40 percent of the millionaires surveyed. Those who have some kind of strong faith exhibit a higher propensity to take financial risks.

CHALLENGE

Spend some time considering the characteristics and qualities of a millionaire mindset discussed in this chapter. What aspects of a millionaire mindset do you recognise in yourself? What are some areas you still need to work on? One of the most important things you need to realise is that you can change. Although you may not know it, the power to change is inside you right now. So tap into it...and change for the better.

[3] Thomas J. Stanley, *The Millionaire Mind,* HarperBusiness, 2000, p.19

CHAPTER 9

money is a tool

Why is it that some people prosper, gain wealth, increase their influence and their capacity to do good, invest successfully, and manage to leave an inheritance for their children and their children's children while others struggle? It's largely a matter of mindset. People can have either a mindset to prosper or a mindset not to prosper. Right thinking will increase your capacity to receive. Wealth is a sign neither of luck nor greed. Most often, it is the result of someone having developed a right mindset and an action plan around money.

It might seem like an obvious statement, but to develop a millionaire mindset, you need to have a positive mindset about money. People can have some pretty silly ideas when it comes to money. In this chapter I want to debunk some of those ideas and help you begin to understand what money is really all about. Money would have to be one of the most controversial and yet misunderstood topics on the planet. We need to shift our mindset and dispel the ridiculous myths about money that have been handed down to us through family, culture, religion or social heritage. Today, you and I need to adopt a new way of thinking about money. We need to have a sound understanding of what money is all about.

Money is an incredible tool, but it's a lousy master. As much as we need to have money in order to achieve anything in life, we also need to be free of money and to hold money lightly. A friend of mine once said, "Some people hold their dollar notes so tight, the Queen starts choking!" (If you are in the United States, it's George Washington that's choking.) It's often said that "money is the root of all evil". This is a misquote from the Bible. The Bible actually says, "The *love of* money is the root of all evil." You can have no money and yet still love it. Conversely, you can have money and yet not love it.

It is amazing to me how many people blame money (or the lack of it) for their problems. Don't blame money or praise money. Money has never broken up a marriage. Money has never done anything of itself. Money is neither good nor bad; it is neither moral nor immoral. It's your attitude towards money and your use of money, not money itself, that determines the effect of money in your life.

> *Money can't make you what you're not already —*
> *money only magnifies what you already are.*

MONEY ONLY MAGNIFIES WHAT YOU ALREADY ARE

Some people think of money as being like a pool. The water in a pool is stagnant. It doesn't move. There is no inlet and no outlet. For them, money must not be spent. My friend, for money to grow, it has to circulate; it must be spread and it must be spent. People save for a rainy day and, sure enough, that is just what they get — a rainy day. Someone once said that money is like manure — if you hoard it, it stinks; if you spread it, it will make things grow! How often do we hear people saying things like, "If I could just win the lotto, or if I could just get a lucky break, then I would support a charity or do some other good with my money"? This is misguided thinking. In actual fact, the person who does not use their money for good when they have small amounts would not be generous with it if they found themselves with big amounts. Money can't make you what you're not already — money only magnifies what you already are.

Some people have said, "If I won a million dollars I would give it all away." That would be foolish. If you won or made a million dollars and you invested it wisely, then over your lifetime you could give away well over a million dollars just out of the interest alone. Margaret Thatcher made this statement about prosperity: "No one would remember the Good Samaritan if he'd only had good intentions — he had money too."

We need to get rid of the 'pie mentality' — the notion that there is only a certain amount of money to go around. How foolish is that way of thinking! Can you imagine if we applied that concept to every area of life? The truth is that there is an abundance of all things in this world — enough for all of us to have abundance. But if we have a 'stagnant pool' mentality about money, we actually clog the flow of prosperity. Be generous with your money, be a giver, be a sharer, and watch what happens — you'll find it will come back to you. If you see money as a stream, rather than a pool, and allow it to flow out from you, then there will always be more flowing back into you.

THE KEY TO WEALTH, PROSPERITY AND MAKING MONEY IS TO SOLVE PROBLEMS

One of the greatest lessons I have ever learnt is that the key to wealth, prosperity and making money is to solve problems. Anyone who has ever created wealth has been in the problem–solving business. People like Bill Gates and Henry Ford have made money because they solved problems. Bill Gates solves information technology problems, Henry Ford solved transportation problems. A good friend of mine once said to me, "Never complain about your troubles, Pat. They are responsible for more than half of your income." That is exactly right! I am in the business of solving problems. Therefore, when I solve problems, I see money as a stream in my life — money comes in and money goes out. I see it as a stream when I invest in the education of others — I put time and money in and it comes back. Norman MacEwan said this: "Happiness is not so much in having or sharing. We make a living by what we get, but we make a life by what we give." Calvin Coolidge said, "No person was ever honoured for what he received; honour has been the reward for what he gave."

Some people are content to have just enough money to get by. I've heard some people say, "I just need enough money to put food on my table." When you think about it, that is a selfish attitude. We need enough money to put food on our table AND someone else's table. Why be content with just enough money to look after your own limited circle of influence? This leads me to another common issue with money: greed. Some people hold on to things very tightly — especially money. Money captures the minds of people because it is one of the most necessary commodities in our lives.

Isn't it amazing how our attitudes surrounding money can change according to the situation? Some people see money as a curse. Others see money as the reason for all their predicaments. For some people, all they see is money. Some people make excuses about money. Some people think they are too virtuous to have a lot of money. Other people often feel a need to apologise for their wealth and well being. But it is not wrong to be wealthy and prosperous. There is no shame in it. Money is not an evil thing — in fact, it is a good thing. What matters is what we do with the money that comes into our world. When money comes to me, it becomes my money. That means it becomes submitted to my ethics, my philosophy and my values.

> *It is what is in the heart of a person that renders that person's money either good or bad.*

Poverty and welfare do not release people into an entrepreneurial spirit. Poverty and welfare keep people controlled, broke, contained, dependent, discouraged and locked in a cycle that continues from generation to generation. The welfare mentality is about giving people handouts. Someone once wisely said that if you give a man a fish you feed him a meal, but if you teach him to fish you feed him for a lifetime.

Money has no mystical or mysterious powers to turn people either into corrupt capitalists or virtuous paupers. It is what is in the heart of a person that renders that person's money either good or bad. The only power that money has is the power you give it. Money takes on the characteristics of the person who has it. In the gambler's hands it will be squandered. In the drug addict's hand it will be used to support bad habits. But in the prosperous person's hand it will be spread about and invested wisely. Money is like electricity — it can be used either to warm something up or to burn something down. In and of itself, money is neither good nor bad. It is just like a kitchen knife, which can be used to carve a piece of roast meat or to stab someone. The knife takes on the characteristics of the person holding it.

CHALLENGE

Do you have negative ideas and attitudes about money? Does the topic of money make you feel uncomfortable? If you want to develop a millionaire mindset, you need to become relaxed about money and see money for what it really is — a wonderful servant in the hands of a master who knows how to control it and to use it to make the world a better place. Money is NOT the root of all evil. As George Bernard Shaw rightly observed, 'the *lack* of money' is a major reason for all kinds of evil in the world today. If you ever want to develop a millionaire mindset, train yourself to think positively about money.

CHAPTER 10

overcome the past from the present to create the future

Everything you need for your future is in embryonic form in your hand today. What do you have in your hand right now? What a tragedy when people constantly lament what they don't have or what has been taken from them. How sad when people lament their losses, rather than celebrate what they have. People lament the loss of innocence at a young age, or a lost relationship, lost money, lost houses or lost businesses. My friend, you can't do a thing about what has been taken from you, but you can do something about whatever it is that you have in your hand right now.

Business owners complain about not having the staff they would like to have, rather than focusing on improving the staff they do have. People complain about not having enough money and talk about what they would be able to do if they had more, rather than doing something constructive with whatever they have right now. It's not what has been taken from you that counts, it's what you do with what you have left over.

Many years ago, one of my closest friends, an honourable man of great integrity, suffered a great injustice through bad information given to him by an accounting firm. It caused him incredible hardship, cost him millions of dollars, and left him bankrupt. As the disaster unfolded, I watched his partners become bitter, disgruntled men. Yet my friend continued to stand tall. He went to his creditors and told them he would pay them everything they were owed. But his partners refused to be involved in any repayment to the creditors. It has been amazing to watch this man resurrect his finances from out of the ashes. How did he do it? He took the little he had left and invested it in knowledge and a new business venture. He realised that what was taken from him didn't matter as much as what he did with what he had left over. Today he is one of the largest franchise owners in Australia and just recently took over the worldwide rights of his ever–expanding franchise business.

Zig Ziglar once said, "Optimists are people who, when they wear out their shoes, just figure they are back on their feet." I think it was Robert Schuller who made the 'glass half full/glass half empty' distinction between an optimist and a pessimist. The optimist pours water into the glass, while the pessimist pours water out of the glass. One looks at what he can put in, the other at what has been taken out. If all you look at is what has been taken out instead of at what is in the glass, then that becomes a dominant mindset in your life and prosperity will not flow.

THE MILLIONAIRE MINDSET MAKES FAILURE A TEACHER

The person who refuses to prosper and looks at what is taken from him makes failure his undertaker. But the millionaire mindset makes failure a teacher. Which will you be? There is a story about a young man who was involved in an oil venture. He eventually ran out of money and sold his interests to his partners. After a lot of time, energy and effort, they finally received a breakthrough and hit a gusher. The company is known today as CITGO. The young man who withdrew later got involved in the clothing business. That turned out worse than his oil venture. It seemed as though a lot had been taken from him. Certainly he had lost a lot; in fact, the man was flat broke. He had a lot to complain about. Yet rather than be discouraged about what he had lost, he became involved in politics. Over the years since, historians have had many wonderful things to say about the great US President, Harry S. Truman. This two–time failure kept his focus on what he had in him that he could use, not on what had been taken from him. Harry S. Truman became the President of the United States not by virtue of what was taken from him, but through what he did with what was left over.

Adversity causes some people to break, but others to break records. Take, for example, the great American athlete, Jesse Owens, who absolutely destroyed the plans of Adolf Hitler with his incredible ability on the athletics track. It was discovered that the reason for his success was an incredible sickness he suffered that caused him to run faster. Then there's the amazing cyclist Lance Armstrong, who fought testicular cancer and yet went on to win the gruelling Tour de France. He recently won his seventh Tour.

Make plans to succeed, not to wallow in your loss.

THE MAJORITY OF MEN MEET WITH FAILURE BECAUSE OF THEIR LACK OF PERSISTENCE

Anyone who wants to prosper and increase, to flourish and advance, must consider what they have now and work on that. Those who are condemned to failure are those who complain about what they have lost, what could have been, might have been or should have been. Such complaining is pointless; it is energy draining and a prosperity thief. If a person's mentality throws up excuses that they were not brought up correctly, or that they'd have been a lot better off if only they'd inherited at least a small amount of wealth to build on, then that person is deceived. Eighty percent of America's millionaires are first generation rich. Two–thirds of them are self–employed; they did not inherit opportunity, they created it from what they had. Napoleon Hill once said, "The majority of men meet with failure because of their lack of persistence in creating new plans, new opportunities to take the place of those that fail."

When you have lost something, stop dwelling on the loss and leverage it to springboard you into a better future. Make plans to succeed, not to wallow in your loss. "But I'm dysfunctional," you may say. Others may say, "I've had my heart broken!" or "I've had a breakdown!" Welcome to the human race, my friend. Everybody has baggage. Everyone has made mistakes. Everyone has been hurt or treated badly at one time or another. If you've messed up or if someone has messed you up at any time in your life, then you are the perfect candidate for success.

GET OVER YOUR PAST

You've got to get over your past. I was once in our national capital at a speaking engagement with over 1,700 young people when a very gothic-looking girl came up to me. She was wearing black from head to foot, her face was painted white and she just looked generally weird. She spoke to me in a gravelly kind of voice: "Can I talk to you?" I have to admit that she freaked me right out! "Sure! Which one of you wants to talk first?" I thought to myself. She showed me her arms and I was horrified — they were cut and slashed all over. It turned out that this girl, Victoria, had been sexually molested between the ages of 7 and 17. She was a mess. But she had a dream. Victoria became involved in our drug and alcohol rehabilitation organisation and went on to help over 70 girls graduate from our program. Today she is a very successful businesswoman. What changed? She had a dream and she got past her past.

Here is some great news: no one has a functional past. We are all, in one way or another, victims of dysfunction. But past mistakes, hurts, fears and failures should be the springboard to your future success. You will learn more from the tragedies of your past than you will ever learn through the good times. You have to get over your past, become bigger than your past, and not dwell in your disappointment about the past. Your prosperity quotient has to be bigger than your disappointment quotient.

Many people get stuck in the past because they are continually looking in the rear vision mirror of their life. You cannot go forward while you are constantly looking backwards. It's like the elephant at the circus. This huge beast is held captive by a small rope and a little stake in the ground. How? Because when the elephant was a baby with very little strength, the circus trainers tied a tiny rope around its ankle and attached the other end to a stake in the ground to keep it from roaming. The elephant never forgets that the stake and the rope prevent it from moving away. Even though it could easily break free, the elephant remains a prisoner of its past. What's your stake in the ground? What's in your past that is holding you captive?

PAST ADVERSITY IS OFTEN THE WINDOW OF OPPORTUNITY

Winston Churchill made this great observation: "Kites rise highest against the wind, not with it." Past adversity is often the window of opportunity for change and betterment. The mind is a filter that enables us to see things. Life is not as it happens; life is how you perceive it. Many people don't prosper because of perceptions based on the past. Other people are able to use the past for their advancement, in spite of tragedy, pain, horror or nightmares from childhood, business dealings or relationships. What makes the difference? The difference is perception. Some people bury the past and move on, other people keep resurrecting a dead corpse. Painful pasts make great building materials for incredible towers of prosperity.

The late Reverend Ross W. Marrs once said this: "Take away my ability to fail and I would not know the meaning of success. Let me be immune to rejection and heartbreak and I could not know the glory of living." Think about that! If you take away the ability to fail, the ability to feel rejection, if you inoculate yourself against heartache and heartbreak, then how are you ever going to become a bigger person?

Painful pasts make great building materials for incredible towers of prosperity.

A few years ago, a friend of mine decided to climb Mount Everest without artificial oxygen. This is what he said to me afterwards: "Pat, the higher I went up that mountain, the less weight I could carry in my knapsack. I got to a point where I went through my knapsack and found my toothbrush and cut the handle off it because all I needed was the head of the toothbrush — I didn't need the excess baggage." He said, "There are some things you just cannot take with you to the top." Don't be comfortable with old problems, be committed to new solutions and prosperity.

It's not only our negative past experiences that can hold us back. There are two kinds of memories in life: good ones and bad ones. And both kinds of memory ruin prosperity. I love this quote from Walt Disney: "I don't like to repeat success, I like to go on to bigger and better things." What a brilliant statement! Bad memories are like chains around our ankles that hinder us from moving forward. Good memories can become hammocks in which we rest.

CHALLENGE

My friend, stop right now and ask yourself this question: "What's in your past that may be holding you captive?" People may have said negative things about you. You may have experienced failures both personally and professionally. But you need to recognise that if you want to go all the way in life, you've got to be prepared to leave the past behind. Only then can you begin to create your future. You see, there are some things you just can't take with you on your journey towards success.

To see prosperity in every area of your life, use the past as building blocks for your advancement. Bury the past and move on. A prosperous person cannot dwell on the past.

CHAPTER 11

know what you want

What do you really want? So often we don't know the answer to this simple yet fundamental question. Many of us declare, "I don't know what I want, but I know what I don't want." This won't get you anywhere. You need to know exactly what you want in life and be able to articulate it and base your life decisions on that knowledge.

In their book *The One Minute Millionaire*, Mark Hansen and Robert Allen relate the story of Sylvester Stallone's struggle to get his first major film role:

> In 1974 Sylvester Stallone was a broke, discouraged actor and screenwriter. While attending a boxing match, he became inspired by a "nobody" boxer who "went the distance" with the great Mohammed Ali.
>
> He rushed home and in a three–day burst of creative output produced the first draft of the screenplay entitled *Rocky.*
>
> Down to his last $106, Stallone submitted his screenplay to his agent. A studio offered $20,000 with either Ryan O'Neal or Burt Reynolds playing the lead character. Stallone was excited by the offer, but wanted to play the lead himself. He offered to act for free. He was told, "That's not the way it works in Hollywood." Stallone

turned down the offer, though he desperately needed the money. Then they offered him $80,000 on the condition that he wouldn't play the lead. He turned them down again.

They told him that Robert Redford was interested, in which case they'd pay him $200,000. He turned them down once more.

They upped their offer to $300,000 for his script. He told them that he didn't want to go through his whole life wondering "what if?"

They offered him $330,000. He told them he'd rather not see the movie made if he couldn't play the lead.

They finally agreed to let him play the lead. He was paid $20,000 for the script plus $340 per week minimum actor's scale. After expenses, agent fees, and taxes, he netted about $6,000 instead of $330,000. In 1976 Stallone was nominated for an Academy Award as Best Actor. The movie *Rocky* won three Oscars: Best Picture, Best Director, and Best Film Editing. The *Rocky* series has since grossed almost $1 billion, making Sylvester Stallone an international movie star![4]

NOTHING WILL HAPPEN UNTIL YOU DECIDE TO PROSPER

Stallone knew what he wanted and was seemingly prepared to make any sacrifice in order to get it. If you want to prosper, you have to focus on what you want. You have to make a choice; you have to make a decision. Nothing happens in life until you make a decision. Your decision could be:

"I'm going to commit to become prosperous!"

"I'm going to commit to create wealth!"

"I'm going to commit to build a great business!"

"I'm going to commit to build a house!"

"I'm going to commit to have a family!"

What do you want? You've got to choose. The singer Gloria Estefan once said, "We seal our fate with the choices we make." What choices have you made about the kind of life you want to have? If you don't know what you want, how will you recognise what you want when you see it? If you're single and you want to be married, have you chosen what kind of spouse you want?

4 Mark Victor Hansen & Robert G. Allen, *The One Minute Millionaire*, Random House, 2002, p.122

I once had a client who wanted to get married. One day I asked her, "What kind of man do you want?"

She replied, "Oh, anyone will do. At my age you can't be too choosy."

I pointed to a rather large and dishevelled character sitting at another table. "What about that guy over there, then? The toothless hairy one," I suggested.

"Oh no!" she quickly replied, "I wouldn't want someone like him."

"Okay," I said. "That's *one* ruled out. So, what kind of man do you want?"

> *Sometimes we just haven't taken the time to think through what it is we actually want.*

If you're married, let me ask you this: what kind of marriage do you want? Every marriage has a culture, a personality (some marriages have the personality of a war zone!). What kind of personality do you want your marriage to have? Every bank account has a personality too. Businesses are the same. Is the personality of your business one of wanting to grow, to increase, to prosper, to invest, to gain knowledge, and to learn? Apply this question to every important area in your world: What kind of business/career/marriage/family/home/lifestyle… do I want?

Sometimes we just haven't taken the time to think through what it is we actually want. We think we kind of know what we want, but we struggle to articulate it. This is a very basic starting point for developing a millionaire mindset. It's really not a difficult question. It's not rocket science. Life is so simple, you have to go to university to mess it up!

What do you want in life? You have to choose. What car do you want to drive? Where do you want to live? Don't go straight to "I can't afford it". Sylvester Stallone couldn't afford to turn down a $20,000 offer for his script (let alone $330,000!). Making up your mind is the first thing. The rest is about time, decision–making, planning, input and growth. But if you don't know clearly what you want, how will you ever get there?

IF YOU AIM FOR NOTHING, THEN YOU'RE BOUND TO HIT IT

Apple co–founder Steve Jobs convinced one–time Pepsi CEO John Scully to take the helm of Apple by asking him, "Do you want to sell sugared water the rest of your life, or do you want a chance to change the world?" Jobs forced Scully to take stock of his present situation and to think about what he really wanted from life. Don't settle for a 'sugared water existence' when in your heart of hearts what you really want is to change the world. My friend, if it's a mist in your mind, it's a fog in your world. If you aim for nothing, then you're bound to hit it!

I was in America once speaking at a large network marketing conference and during a break in sessions I went to get a coffee. (Whenever I'm away, I always go looking for a good espresso!) I was on my way to the coffee shop when a rather large African–American gentleman came up to me and asked me if I had any change. I said to him, "Do you want change or do you want dollars?"

He looked at me, surprised, and said, "Are you jivin' me, man?"

"No, I'm not jivin' you," I said. "I want to know what you really want."

"I want to get some food," he replied.

"Oh, so you really want food?" I said.

"Yeah, I want to buy some food. I figure if you've got some change I can get myself a sandwich," he explained.

I said, "I'll tell you what, how about I buy you your whole meal?"

This idea seemed to appeal to him. "Yeah, alright man!" he said. "You from Australia?"

"Yes."

"I always wanted to go to Australia." (Now there's a millionaire mindset — he couldn't afford a meal, but he dreamed of flying to Australia!)

So I took the man to a deli and bought him a whole heap of food. Then I gave him $10. He thanked me and we went our separate ways.

The very next day, I was in the lobby of my hotel when another man came into the lobby and approached me. "You got some change?" he asked me.

So I said, "Do you want change or do you want dollars?"

"I want to get some food," he said.

"Great!" I replied. "Let me take you down to the deli and I'll buy you a meal." (By then I knew where the deli was!)

He said, "No, no! Just give me the money!"

Now, I was born at night, but not last night, so I said, "No, no, no! If you want food, I'll buy you food."

"I just need some change, man!" he replied.

Again I asked him, "Do you want change or do you want dollars?"

"I just want some money," he said, getting frustrated. Then he walked away.

I watched him as he walked out of the hotel lobby and approached a lady outside who happened to be one of the conference delegates. He asked her for some change and she offered him some food — a sandwich and some fruit that she had just bought. Incredibly, he refused it, saying, "No, I don't want it!"

Funny, isn't it, how you can think you want something, but when it's offered to you, you knock it back because you really don't know what you want.

DO YOU KNOW WHAT YOU WANT IN LIFE?

What do you really want in life? I recently put this question to a group of real estate professionals. These people were high–income earners. Their response to my question was that it's a very hard question to answer. I disagreed. You see, I know what I want in life, and if I can figure it out, so can you. I want to prosper. I want to create wealth. I want to help other people become wealthy. I want to help people who are disadvantaged go to another level, and to do that I need money.

I was once in Orange County in California and I was asked by a friend to visit a young man named Steve in hospital. He was dying from AIDS. He was only 19 years old, but when I walked into his room and saw him for the first time, he looked like a 95–year–old man. He had lesions on his face and one side of his face was black and blue. His eye on his dark side was shut tight and he was having difficulty breathing. The nurse helped him to sit up and we were introduced.

"How are you going, Steve?" I asked him.

"Not good," he replied in a weak, husky voice.

I asked, "Is the medication helping?"

He said, "No, medication's not helping."

This young man was dying in front of me. Then he looked at me and said, "A minister came in here yesterday and prayed for us all to get healed."

Now, I believe things like that happen. I believe in miracles. So I asked him, "Did anybody get healed?"

He looked at me and I could see his anger through the pain on his black and blue face. "No, man," he said. "Nobody got healed."

Then I asked the dumbest question in all of human history: "Steve, do you want to get healed?"

I'll never forget what he said next as he turned to me and his open eye went red as a tear began to form.

"No, man," he said, "I don't want to be healed. I just want to be loved."

Steve knew what he wanted, even though other people assumed he wanted something else. For the last six weeks of Steve's life, my friend and members of his community surrounded Steve with love.

WHAT DOES YOUR WORLD LOOK LIKE?

I used to run programs to help rehabilitate drug addicts and we had an 86 percent success rate using these techniques. If it can work for them, it can work for you! I'd ask them the question, "What does your world look like?" and they'd reply, "Well, I'm free of drugs and I'm happy and I'm getting on with my mum and dad and my mum's hugging me..." The theme of our program was 'turning nightmares into dreams'.

I remember one day a lady came into our facility and I asked her if I could help her.

She said, "I've come to pick up my dream."

It didn't immediately occur to me what she meant. I said, "You're here to pick up your dream?" (I thought perhaps she was interested in me!).

"Yes," she said. "My son, Robbie. He came in here nine months ago and he was a nightmare. Now he has graduated. He has become a dream. Where is he? Where's my dream? Where's my boy?" (Such beautiful words!)

The only thing we really had to do with some of those guys was to get them to think differently. There are plenty of detox centres in my city with a low 14 percent success rate. The truth is, we don't have a drug problem, we have a vision problem. Adults tell young people, "Don't expect much out of life" or "Well, your father was an alcoholic so what else would you expect?" or "The apple doesn't fall far from the tree." This kind of mindset is nothing but lies that rob people of their future. I can assure you that I fell a long way from my family tree! I was sling–shot out of my tree!

Here is something else I want: I have recently started a club called The Millionaire Mindset Club. I want to help 10,000 people become millionaires, or at least to help them start thinking like a millionaire. That's what I want. And you too can become a part of this club.

If we haven't decided what we want, then there is no point in having a plan. People often start planning before they've figured out what they want.

"I'm planning for my future," someone may say.

"What does your future look like?" I would ask.

"I don't know," they'll say.

"Then how can you plan for it?"

My friend, if you're planning to play a game of football, but you don't know where the game is being played, then how can you possibly turn up to play? If you don't know where the goalposts are, how can you score?

CHALLENGE

Pause for a moment and ask yourself these questions:

What do you want?

Do you want to prosper?

Do you want to create wealth?

Do you want to build a great business?

Do you want to have a loving family?

Do you want to give lots of money to people in need?

To help people work through these questions, I often use focus sheets. I ask people, "If your life was a blank canvas in front of you, what would you want to put on it?" It's amazing how many people don't know.

Now if I was to give you a blank canvas and I asked you to close your eyes and paint a picture in your mind of what you'd like your life to look like, what would you paint? What's your family like? What are your kids like? What's your career like? What's your world like?
If your world was ideal, what would it look like? How would you think? How would you feel? How would you speak? How would you live?

The title of this chapter is 'Know What You Want'. If you don't make up your mind, your unmade–up mind will make itself up for you. Don't get to the end of your life and wonder, "How did I get here?" Everybody ends up somewhere, whether they mean to or not. Make sure you end up somewhere on purpose. When you know what you want, then you can start to make your plans.

CHAPTER 12

you need to focus

Focus is a discipline and, as such, it needs to be developed. To have a millionaire mindset, we need to learn how to keep our minds focused on whatever it is that we want. Your mind is like a muscle. Just as regular exercise and physical exertion build and strengthen our muscles, the mind is strengthened by focus. For muscles to grow, they must be exercised and fed. You have to focus on them in order for them to increase. If you want to see increased wealth or progress in any area of your life, you must keep your focus on what you want and not allow distractions to rule you. Whatever you feed will grow, and whatever you starve will die. Successful people know how to keep their focus firmly and clearly on their desired ends.

My mother was a wonderful woman. As a child, I remember that as I would go out to play with my friends, my mother would call after me, "Pasquale, pay attention when you cross the road. If you get hit by a truck, don't you come crying to me! Pay attention!"

I also remember how one of my teachers, Mrs Bird, would come up behind me in class while I was busy daydreaming and she would slam her hand down on my desk and shout, "Pat Mesiti! Pay attention!" My mother and Mrs Bird both understood a powerful principle in developing a millionaire mindset: the principle of focus.

Once you've figured out exactly what you want, the next challenge is to stay focused on it. It is impossible to achieve what you want if your attention is constantly being distracted all over the place. Focus requires specialisation. We need to stay with our main game. Focus gives you an edge, because the longer you work at something, the better you get at it. Focus is made up of a number of factors:

F – Forward planning

O – Overcoming distractions

C – Committing to a plan

U – Understanding your objectives

S – Sustaining effort

Whatever you feed will grow, and whatever you starve will die. Successful people know how to keep their focus firmly and clearly on their desired ends.

Forward planning: Know exactly what you want in life. Begin to plan how it is going to happen. Have a long–term and medium–term plan, but also have a plan for today. If you don't plan your day, your day will have a mind of its own. Think what needs to be done today to keep you on track. Then stick to your plan.

Overcoming distractions: Anything that draws your attention away from what you are trying to achieve is a distraction. Life is full of them. What are the things that easily distract you? Be aware of what the main distractions are in your life. Understand your propensity to be distracted. What is it that typically distracts you at the most important time? Be alert and prepare yourself not to be distracted. Wherever possible, remove the source of distraction.

Committing to a plan: Be committed to your plan. Keep yourself accountable. Make a 'to do' list and prioritise everything on it. Someone once said they often feel like a mosquito at a nudist colony — so much to do but they don't know where to start! There is always a lot to do. Prioritise what you need to do, make a plan to get it done, and commit to your plan.

Understanding your objectives: As well as knowing 'what', we also need to know 'why'. In my own life, it's not just a matter of knowing that I want to be prosperous, it's also about knowing why I want to be prosperous. Know the answer to the questions "Why am I here?" and "What am I here to do?" Have clearly defined objectives.

Sustaining effort: Nothing worthwhile comes without significant effort. Anything worth having is worth working for. As a well-known advertisement says, "It won't happen overnight, but it will happen." Don't give up. Don't get discouraged. Keep working at it — that's what leads to success.

FOR LASTING CHANGE, WE HAVE TO STAY FOCUSED ON OUR GOAL

At the drug rehabilitation centre I used to run, young men would come in saying, "I want to get off drugs." Then we'd give them the briefing. For the next nine months, their lives would belong to us and they'd be subjected to a very intense and highly regimented daily routine involving a lot of hard work and personal discipline. After hearing about what was going to be required of them, some of them thought, "I don't think I want to get off drugs now." For real and lasting change to happen in our lives, we have to be prepared to stay focused on our goal. If you want to be prosperous, you have to stay focused on the things that will lead you into prosperity. It's amazing how many people change their perspective or lose their desire because they lose focus. Ultimately, your life will go in the direction of your focus.

Sometimes when I travel I get back cramps. I was once in Singapore when I went to Lucky Plaza where there is a group of shops that sell electronic goods. One salesman was selling an electronic massager that you can wear as pads on your body. "This is very good for massage," he informed me. "But only use it for ten minutes a day — very dangerous." He pulled out a photo of Bruce Lee. "Bruce Lee used this machine to build muscle," he said.

I was sold! "Give me two of those," I said.

On the plane back to Sydney, I thought to myself, "I have a seven-hour flight from Singapore to Sydney. I can look like Bruce Lee by the time I get off the plane." So I went into the lavatory and placed the electronic pads onto my stomach under my shirt. I was travelling with one of my daughters on that flight. We'd been upgraded, so there I was, sitting next to my unsuspecting daughter with a glass of champagne in my hand.

Now, there were three levels of intensity on the massage machine: low, medium and high. Those people who know me know that I am not a low intensity kind of person. And to me, 'medium' is another word for average, and I never want to be that! So I went straight to the 'high' setting. So I pushed the power button...All of a sudden I was screaming in agony and crying, "Someone take this machine off me!!" Needless to say, my daughter was mortified. Her only comment was, "I'm so not here!" I learned a very important lesson on that flight. You see, I wanted the Bruce Lee six–pack without having to focus on getting it. I'm into down–sizing — instead of the six–pack, I've chosen a one–pack! I've learned that focus involves time and sustained effort; there are no shortcuts.

Once, when I was building a home, I took it upon myself to plant some gardens around my house. But then I didn't look after them and they didn't grow very well. One day I was complaining to some friends about how poor the soil was.

"I planted these plants a year ago and they're not growing," I told them.

"Have you tried watering them?" one of my friends asked.

What a novel idea! I had wanted abundance, fruitfulness and prosperity in my garden, but I hadn't been diligent enough to focus on what it would take to achieve that.

FOCUS HELPS US OVERCOME OBSTACLES

Focus can be incredibly powerful. It can help us to overcome seemingly insurmountable obstacles and bring about change in the face of what might seem like overwhelming adversity. I recall a young 10–year–old boy in New York City called Jason who was living on the streets. His story was horrific. His mother's 'lover' had carved his name in Jason's skin. Everything within Jason was focused on revenge. His constant thought was, "I'm going to kill that guy!" Everything in his environment — his home life and his culture — said he would probably do just that. What he needed was for someone to help him see that he had a choice. I said to him, "Jason, you can do that. Or you can choose to do something with your life." What Jason needed to do was to shift his focus from his past to his future. As Henry Ford once said, "If you think you can or you think you can't, you're right." Today, Jason is a successful young attorney in New York City.

I was once talking to a woman who had had seven marriages (she was obviously very good at it!). I asked her, "What is the one thing those seven marriages had in common?" Her answer was very telling.

"Men!" she said. "Abusive men."

I knew there was something else going on here, so I asked her to tell me her history. It turned out that she had been brought up by an abusive alcoholic father. Then when she'd grown up, she met a guy who had a few challenges, but she thought she'd sort him out once she married him. So she ended up marrying an abusive, alcoholic wife–beater. She eventually got divorced and then married one of his friends. (What is it they say about 'birds of a feather'?) Over the following years, every one of her husbands was an abusive man. After hearing her story, I asked her this question: "When are you going to stop trying to rescue daddy?" That's what she was trying to do. She was focused on her experience with her father and her life was following the direction of her focus. Be aware of where your wrong thinking comes from.

LEARN TO VALUE RESULTS

We live in a results–oriented culture. People will generally judge you or accept you on the basis of one thing: results. Prosperity is about results. If I didn't know how to prosper and have some results, I wouldn't be in a position to write this book. I have learnt to value results. I want results. Sometimes someone might say something like, "I just want to be happy." But what does that mean? Where's the tangible result in that? Others will say, "I want peace…" What does that mean? We need to define what we want so that there is a measurable result attached to it. Otherwise, how will we know when we've achieved our goals?

If you are married or in a long–term relationship, remember how much you focused when you were first dating your partner? You even had a shower before you went out! Remember how you opened and closed the car door, and how you remembered her birthday and even her mother's birthday? Remember how you fell in love with him and dreamt of running along the beach in slow motion together? Then he asked the big question and you said "yes". Next there was the honeymoon — there was a lot of focus then! Seven years later, he has become the fastest remote controller in town! Three kids later, she has stopped caring about how she looks. Somehow, over the years you've both lost your focus. Or you've stopped focusing on all the things that brought you together and instead you're focusing on all the things that will keep you apart.

I was once helping a married couple who were doing just that — they were focusing on everything that was wrong and fighting tooth and nail. I took them into separate rooms and told each of them to write down on a piece of paper what it was that they had loved about the other before they were married. Then I brought them back into the same room and sat them down facing each other. I told him to tell her what he'd written. Before he could get through about five or six points, he became all teary, and she was a mess too. Then I told her to tell him what she had written. She was too emotional to get through the list.

WHATEVER YOU FOCUS ON WILL PROGRESS

Focus on what's right, not on what's wrong. Whatever you focus on will progress and whatever you neglect will regress. Many people get sick because they neglect their bodies through smoking, poor eating habits, lack of exercise, or not enough sleep. But a change of focus can turn around years of neglect. If someone in poor physical condition decides they want to be healthy and then gets focused on becoming healthy, then change will happen. As they give up smoking, start eating well, begin exercising regularly and generally begin to live a wholesome lifestyle, their physical condition begins to improve. Why? Because you get what you focus on.

So often we create around ourselves an environment of neglect. Consider for a moment the room you are in right now. I'm assuming that your room is in a reasonable state of order, cleanliness and repair. But if you were simply to leave the room right now and not come back into it for a number of years, do you think that room would be in the same condition on your return? Of course not. There will be dust everywhere, the furniture and curtains will have faded, the paint may have started flaking here and there, and there will probably be some evidence of vermin around the room. The room's condition will have deteriorated simply through neglect. It's the same with our lives. If we neglect some part of our world, then that area will regress. So many people fail to focus on what they want and they do nothing about it. Then later they wonder why they always seem to be going backwards in life.

We need to destroy the mind viruses that are crippling us. One of the most prevalent mental afflictions is called 'distraction'. Distraction is the number one enemy of focus. There are so many things out there vying for your attention, but most of them are nothing more than distractions that will take your focus off the things you should be giving your attention to.

Thomas Fuller, chaperone of Charles II of England, once observed, "He that is everywhere is nowhere." In order to achieve anything, you need to focus on a target. Distractions put distance between you and your goal. They interrupt your progress. They cause you to stray from the path that is leading you to your goals. They encourage your mind to wander. They lead you into forming bad habits and reverting to old habits that will hold you back. They cause you to expend your energy non–productively. They make you time poor. Above all, they destroy your focus.

Another enemy of focus is the 'I want results and I want them now' mindset. Now, 99.9 percent of the time that's not how things work. Focus involves time, effort, energy and input. It requires that you be single–minded. If you desire financial growth, business growth, success growth, wealth growth or relational growth but you are not prepared to put in the necessary time and effort to develop your mind muscle through sustained focus on your desired goals, then you will hinder your progress towards prosperity.

THE ENVIRONMENT SURROUNDING YOUR MIND WILL DETERMINE YOUR SUCCESS

If you want prosperity in your life, you have to start focusing. You need to create an environment for focus in your life. Your mind will function better if you create the right environment around it. You see, the environment you create around your mind will determine your success. Removing or learning to ignore distractions is part of this process. But you also need to put in place in your world certain practices and principles that will develop an environment around you that is conducive to staying focused and to sharpening your mind.

You have to get your mind under control. Your mind is your greatest asset. Give it some attention. Most people's income shrinks to the level of their mindset. Focus on putting some stuff in your mind that will enlarge your mindset. My car is a rolling university of success. Whenever I'm on the road, I listen to successful people teaching me about success. I'm always reading too. I always have a book in my briefcase. If you want to prosper, you have to learn to think a certain way.

Feed your mind with the kind of material that will help keep you focused. How many books do you read each month? How much motivational or educational material do you listen to? Do you have success mentors helping you to create an environment for wealth creation around your mind? In what ways are you developing and strengthening your mind so that when wealth and prosperity come your way, you will know exactly what to do? You have to focus on creating an environment around you that encourages and promotes the pursuit of success and prosperity.

In what ways are you developing and strengthening your mind so that when wealth and prosperity come your way, you will know exactly what to do?

You will never possess something that you are unwilling to pursue. Focus requires clarity and specificity. You need to be pursuing not just some abstract ideal but something tangible — a specific amount, a certain type of relationship, a certain position or opportunity. Think about what kind of people you want to have in your world. Even go as far as thinking about which specific individuals with whom you'd like to build an association.ursue relationships with people who are ahead of you, more skilled thanyou, more intelligent that you, and more creative than you. Being around people like that will help take you to another level.

FOCUS IS ABOUT RELENTLESS PURSUIT

Prosperity has to be actively pursued. That's what focus is all about — relentless pursuit. Here are a few general things you must focus on pursuing in order to become more prosperous:

- Excellence
- Integrity
- The wellbeing of others
- Positive acquaintances
- Knowledge

Another important principle in developing focus is to pay attention to your attitudes. One particular trap to watch out for is the trap of complacency. Many people who have reached a certain level of success make the mistake of becoming familiar or comfortable with their success or their level of success. They say familiarity breeds contempt. But in this context, familiarity breeds regression and failure. Familiarity can manifest in a number of ways — as arrogance, as over confidence, as a loss of passion, a lack of care, or as presumption. Great sports people or teams are often beaten by relatively lowly ranked opposition because of familiarity.

Focus also requires that we have an understanding of the 'big picture'. While it's important to stay focused on the details and the small things that may seem insignificant, ultimately no one is motivated by details. It's the big picture that keeps us motivated. In my book *Attitudes and Altitudes*, I speak about the difference between 'whats' and 'whys'. 'Whats' are the tasks you have to do to pursue prosperity — the calls you need to make, the people you need to meet, the books you need to read, the deals you need to close, and so on. Often the 'whats' can be menial or mundane. That's why the 'whys' are so important. The 'whys' are all about vision. They are what drive you and motivate you. You need to stay focused on the big picture. You need to have a grand vision that provides a broad context for every decision, every choice and every strategy along the way. Your vision also provides a framework for learning and for your relationships.

LOOK AT THE BIG PICTURE, BUT DON'T IGNORE THE DETAILS

So focus is all about maintaining an awareness of the big picture while simultaneously not taking your eyes off the details. Alvin Poplar put it this way: "You have got to think about the big things while you are doing the small things so that all the small things go in the right direction."

In his book *Thinking for a Change*, Dr John C. Maxwell makes some great points about unleashing the potential of focused thinking. He identifies the following benefits of maintaining focus:

- Focus harnesses energy towards a desired goal
- Focus gives ideas time to develop
- Focus brings clarity to the target
- Focus will take you to the next level

Focus means sticking with something to its completion. Harry A. Overstreet once stated, "The immature mind hops from one thing to the other; the mature mind seeks to follow through." It requires discipline and concentration. As Bertrand Russell said, "To be able to concentrate for a considerable time is essential to difficult achievement."

Focus means sticking with something to its completion.

In his book, *Focus — The Future of Your Company Depends On It*, Al Ries offers this great illustration of the difference between focus and lack of focus. The sun is a powerful source of energy. Every hour the sun washes the earth with billions of kilowatts of energy. Yet with a hat and some sunscreen, you can bathe in the light of the sun for hours at a time with few ill effects. A laser, on the other hand, is a weak source of energy. A laser takes a few watts of energy and focuses them in a coherent stream of light. But with a laser you can drill a hole in a diamond or wipe out a cancer. That's the power of focus. Unleash the power of focused thinking and you will reap the results.

CHALLENGE

Start focusing now if you want prosperity in your life. Discipline your mind. Recognise distractions when they come your way and resist them. Realise that your mind is your greatest asset. Give it some attention. Feed it with great books and positive audio tapes. Whenever you are in your car, listen to successful people teach you principles and attitudes of success. If you want a higher income, a better marriage, or a larger business, then you have to learn to think a certain way. So make a decision today to start focusing!

To develop a millionaire mindset, you need to stay focused on creating wealth, focused on prosperity, focused on your business, or focused on creating the right kind of thinking about yourself and your world.

Here are seven key areas of focus that I believe are important for anyone aspiring to become prosperous:

- Focus on yourself.
- Focus on your communication skills — including your posture, your facial expressions, your tact and diplomacy, and your attitude.
- Focus on your area of expertise — become an expert at what you do best.
- Focus on knowing people — your client base, for example. Know what motivates them. Know their dreams and desires, and know what they want from life.
- Focus on your strengths — maximise your effectiveness. A few years ago, the USA and China faced off in the world table tennis championships. The Chinese won overwhelmingly. When they interviewed the coach of the Chinese team afterwards, they asked him how it was that his team was able to beat the opposition so convincingly. He said the difference was in what the two teams focused on. He observed that the Americans' approach was to find someone with a good backhand and train him to try and have a good forehand, whereas the Chinese approach was to take a player with a good backhand and match

him up with someone who had a good forehand so they could work off each other's strengths. In other words, they focused on their strengths, not their weaknesses.

- Focus on follow–through — one of the greatest keys to success is following up clients and following up on what you said you would do.
- Focus on developing momentum — momentum creates and builds energy for future success.
- Focus on being persuasive — people are persuaded when you show them how *they* will be advantaged, not how you will be advantaged. To create wealth and prosperity you must learn the art of positive persuasion. This requires focus.

Developing a millionaire mindset requires a focused mind. Spend some time each day forcing yourself to focus your mind on the things that matter in your world.

CHAPTER 13

pay attention to growth

Many people try to achieve success by making cosmetic changes. But the reality is that only inner improvements will lead to outer improvements. Only with real changes to our mindsets and attitudes will real results be seen. At the end of the last chapter 'Focus on yourself' was at the top of the list of things we need to focus on. What do I mean by this? Well, you need to focus on your own personal growth and development. This will help you to prepare for maximum effectiveness. Abraham Lincoln once said, "If it takes eight hours to cut down a tree, I'd spend seven hours sharpening the axe." You see, you need to sharpen your mind first in order to see effective success in business, career and relationships.

You need to pay attention to your growth. For instance, make sure there's always something in your tank. If you're running on empty, you'll find yourself syphoning up trash from the bottom of your tank. But if you're full, you will always be able to give something back. In order to give something away, you first need to have a surplus. This applies to a whole range of things, whether it is money or something less tangible, such as experience. For example, how can I teach other people about how to become successful and prosperous if I don't have a wealth of personal experience in these areas? Someone might say to me, "I want to be a motivational speaker like you." My reply would be, "Well, what have you achieved to provide a background of experience from which you can impart to others?"

Without struggle, we don't gain strength.
Without pain, we don't progress.

To have anything to give, there has to be something of value within us. Regardless of religious beliefs, I'm sure everyone would have to agree that one of the most powerful speakers on the planet is Dr Billy Graham. He is an amazing communicator. Even today in his latter years he is still able to gather enormous crowds and hold people's attention with his authority. When Dr Graham speaks, people listen. Some new upstart preacher could get up and give the same message as Dr Graham, and yet he wouldn't attract the same attendance or the same attention. Why do they listen to Dr Graham? Because he has a wealth of experience; he has weight.

This kind of experience only comes our way through constant exposure to challenges. Without challenge, we don't grow. Without struggle, we don't gain strength. Without pain, we don't progress.

GROWTH IS A PROCESS, NOT AN EVENT

If you want progress in your life, you've got to pay attention to your growth. You see, growth is a process, not an event. "Yes, but I went to one seminar years ago and it changed my life," someone may say. There's always going to be much more to it than that. A seminar might get you kick–started, but it's how you proceed from that start that really makes the difference. People will sometimes come up to me and ask, "What's the one book I need to read?" Again, one book or one CD can be enough to get you started, but lasting change is an ongoing process.

Prosperity is a process. Some people win lotto and within a few years all the money is gone. Why? Because their wealth was the result of an event, not a process. They never learned how to be prosperous. They never developed a millionaire mindset. They suddenly found they had a lot of money, but there was no process of growth to learn how to handle wealth.

We all need to grow — in our relationships, in what we believe, in what we know, in knowing what we are capable of doing, and in our understanding of ourselves. (It has taken me 45 years just to start to understand myself, and I still haven't got it totally figured out!)

It's important to understand that you are responsible for your own growth and development, but not anyone else's. Sometimes we can tend to think that the changes that need to happen in our world depend on people around us changing. You may have heard the story of the man who came home drunk night after night, causing his wife all kinds of grief and disruption. Finally this wonderful, patient woman had had enough. In her frustration, she decided to do something about it. She went to a costume shop and hired a red devil suit and a pitchfork. She decided she would try to scare him into changing his drunken ways. When he arrived home late that night, drunk as usual, she jumped out in front of him screaming and holding the pitchfork in front of him. Her husband merely looked at her and said, "You don't scare me — I married your sister!"

GROWTH HAPPENS BY CHOICE, NOT BY COERCION

Generally speaking, bribes and threats — carrots and sticks — do not motivate us to grow. Growth happens by choice, not by coercion. Prosperity comes by choice, not by chance. Fear, threats and bribes might motivate you for a while, but they won't have long–term effects. Growth requires focus. It is determined by what you surround yourself with and what you feed into your mental, spiritual and emotional bank account. Merely desiring growth is not enough; there has to be change. Growth equals change and change equals growth.

Prosperity comes by choice, not by chance.

Many people don't grow in life. They always have the same problems. For them, nothing ever changes or progresses. A man once came up to me and said, "Pat Mesiti, I'm sick of all your happy claptrap stuff." His wife was standing behind him looking embarrassed. He continued, "I've had 20 years of experience. What could you know that I don't?"

I said to him, "Sir, you haven't had 20 years of experience, you've had one experience over and over for 20 years. And as a result you're miserable, you're tight, and you're poor."

His wife was standing behind him cheering me on! You see, he had never grown. He just kept doing the same thing year in and year out and nothing ever changed. His life was like a treadmill — he was walking through life, but he wasn't going anywhere. Some people never graduate from the kindergarten of life. Their wealth never grows because their mindsets stay small and limited.

Here's an example of something very practical you can do to help your personal growth, to help develop your millionaire mindset: next time you go out to a restaurant for dinner, go to one that's just a bit nicer than the kind of restaurant you would normally go to. And when you go to that nice restaurant, don't look down at the menu and say to your spouse, "Honey, get the chicken. It's the cheapest thing on the menu." I recently came home from a trip and my wife, Andrea, picked me up from the airport. I told her to book any restaurant she liked for dinner that night (what was I thinking!). Needless to say, it turned out to be an expensive night, but it was a great night!

When you buy your wife flowers and there is a choice between a $15 bunch of roses that looks okay and a $40 bunch that looks beautiful, don't think to yourself, "Well, she doesn't know there are two bunches, so she won't know the difference." She'll know alright! Every now and then you should try on a millionaire mindset for size. Go on — I dare you! You never know, you might find it fits better than you think!

Growth has nothing to do with your age; it is all about your desire for success. The prosperous person grows into his or her prosperity. Build your life in increments. When you've worked out what you want, start moving your life towards it. One change makes way for the next change, creating the opportunity for us to grow. Your growth is determined by a number of factors.

Here are three things that I believe will help you grow in order to attain greater prosperity:

- **Emotional implantation** – You need someone in your life who will encourage you and help you to see what you can't see and what can be done.

- **Repetition** – Develop growth habits.
- **Discomfort** – This is the real determining factor. Discomfort will cause you to grow. For your muscles to grow, they must experience a level of discomfort. You will learn more in adversity than you will ever learn when things are going well. It is what you believe and how you act in your worst moment that determines what you really believe and who you really are.

CHALLENGE

Here are 10 'A's of personal growth — 10 straightforward and simple strategies that can help you move beyond average growth into exponential growth, wealth creation and prosperity.

1. **ANALYSE.** Growth starts by analysing exactly where you are right now. Analyse your current situation. Where are you now? Are you in a place of contentment or are you hungry for something more? If you go to a doctor and she gives you a wrong diagnosis (analysis), you won't be able to treat the problem effectively. It's the same when it comes to personal growth.

2. **AIM.** Set your sights on where you want to be. Most people run their lives on the principle of 'ready, fire, aim'. To move ahead, you need to aim correctly first. Many people shoot at anything — they have no specific target. Instead of taking aim, they randomly fire away, putting bullet holes in walls. Then they take a crayon and draw a target around one of the bullet holes and call it a bullseye. That is not a bullseye; it's a whole lot of bull!

3. **ADJUST.** Be ready to make adjustments as you go. If you find you are not heading in the direction you want to be going or experiencing the kind of growth you are hoping for, then you must change direction now. There's a story about a large battleship that was ploughing through heavy seas with low visibility when it received an urgent message: "Adjust your course. You are heading for a collision."

The captain of the ship sent a stern reply: "I know exactly where I am heading. Adjust your course!"

The voice came back over the radio, "Adjust your course. Danger is imminent!"

The captain grabbed the microphone: "If you want to avoid a collision, adjust *your* course! I am a battleship!"

Back came one final cool reply: "If you want to avoid a collision, adjust *your* course. I am a lighthouse!"

If you are heading in a direction that is not leading you into growth, be flexible, learn how to swallow your pride, and adjust your course!

4. **ALIGN.** Align yourself with the right people. Align yourself with people who will stretch you and who can teach you; people who will challenge your thinking, your mindset and your motivation. Align yourself with people who will change your perception of things and who have already been where you want to go. If you are earning $100,000 a year, hang around people earning a million dollars a year. If you are a millionaire, hang around billionaires.

5. **AFFIRM**. Affirmation is important to growth. Affirm your dream. Affirm your core beliefs. Affirm yourself. Affirm others.

6. **ANTICIPATE**. Anticipate growth. Anticipate productivity. Remember, your mind and your wealth will go in the direction of your focus. Your life will follow your focus. If you anticipate opportunity, prosperity and growth, then that's what you'll get.

7. **APPLY**. Apply truths and apply what you really believe. Apply what you know. I recall the story of a tightrope walker named Blondin who, to the amazement of a large crowd gathered at the top of Niagara Falls, succeeded in walking a tightrope suspended across the huge thundering waterfall. On his way back across the falls, the people cheered and clapped, "Blondin! Blondin! Blondin!" He asked the crowd if they believed he could do it again. They cheered louder and they clapped

harder. Then he asked if anyone was prepared to sit in a wheelbarrow and let him wheel them across the rope. The crowd fell silent. Everyone believed, but no one wanted to apply their belief! You need to apply and practise what you believe to achieve personal growth.

8. **ADOPT**. Adopt the right habits. They will help you grow into the person you want to be.

9. **ABANDON**. Abandon bad habits, abandon negativity, abandon bad relationships and abandon old mindsets so that you can replace the old with the new.

10. **ACCELERATE**. Put your foot down and accelerate your growth. Growth is forward motion. To grow, we have to accelerate and move forward. Accelerate beyond difficulties, excuses, what the market is telling you, and accelerate towards your future growth.

We need to be pregnant with growth. When you are pregnant with growth, eventually you will give birth to new things. You can also grow by learning from your mistakes. Mistakes are events. They don't have to become a permanent condition of your life.

CHAPTER 14

the power of decision making

There are some things in life you don't get to decide on. Your birthday, for example. You don't get to decide when to be born. You sometimes hear people express this realisation: "I didn't ask to be born!" Generally speaking, we don't get to decide how or when we die either. But we have a lot of choice about what happens in between these two events. We can choose how we live.

Without a doubt, there are things that happen to us in life that are beyond the power of our decisions. Some people are abused or treated badly by their parents or other people in their lives. I've met young men whose lives have been totally devastated because their fathers had committed suicide when they were young boys. Did these young guys choose that? No. But while we may not have any power of decision over how people hurt us, abuse us, desert us or let us down, we do have the power to choose to move on from these experiences and not allow them to rule our lives. These are the choices we need to make. A millionaire mindset is a mindset that decides that the circumstances of the past life will not necessarily determine the future.

A poverty mindset thinks like this: "Life just happens to me. This is my lot and I just have to live with it." A millionaire mindset thinks like this: "Well, that may have been my lot, but I'm going to create a different world for myself." You need to decide to create your future. The greatest ability you have as a human being is the ability to choose, to decide. We must decide to take charge of our lives.

CHOICES ARE EASY IF YOU KNOW WHAT YOU VALUE

How do we make decisions? We need to choose and refuse. We choose the things that are good for us and we refuse the things that are not good for us. When you get married, you choose the person you are marrying and you refuse all others (if you know what's good for you!). We choose according to what we value. What do you value? If you know what you value, choices are easy.

A little while ago, I was staying in a hotel in Auckland, New Zealand, and I was sitting having dinner on my own. I'm no great stud (I'm more like a garden gnome on steroids), but as I was sitting there in my suit having dinner, a rather attractive woman came up to me. Now, I have dinner with people all the time, whether male or female. I'm not particularly paranoid about this as a rule. But there are exceptions to the rule. I feel comfortable with most people, but some give me a kind of vibe. This woman was in the latter camp. She asked me if I was staying in the hotel.

"Yes, I am," I said.

"Are you dining alone?"

"Yes, I am."

"Can I join you for dinner?"

I changed my reply. "No," I said.

"Why not?" she asked.

"Because I'm having dinner on my own, as you just asked me," I politely explained.

She seemed somewhat taken aback at my refusal. "Let me get this straight," she said. "You don't want me to have dinner with you?"

I said, "There's nothing I'd like more than to have dinner with you. However, I've actually met you before."

She was surprised. "No, you haven't," she said.

"Yes, I have," I replied.

She started trying to place me. "Well, what do you do for a living?"

"I'm a speaker," I replied.

"Was I at a conference you were speaking at?" she asked.

At this point, I didn't answer her question directly. "I even know your name," I said.

"You know my name? What's my name then?" she asked.

"Trouble," I replied.

She laughed appreciatively. "That's very funny. So can I have dinner with you?"

"No," I said.

Now, I could have had dinner with her and it wouldn't have been wrong, but it wouldn't have been appropriate. Why? Because I value my wife and my marriage. I made a decision based not on the circumstances of my immediate situation, but on the basis of values and priorities that I have predetermined and on which I maintain my focus. We all make mistakes from time to time. But we need to make decisions that are based on what we value. What do you value? Figure out what's important to you, stay focused on it, and make your decisions accordingly.

Your decisions will either strengthen or weaken your focus. What you focus on will progress. Progress is a result of a concentrated effort in the right direction. Progress happens by choice, not by chance. We choose to keep moving ahead by the decisions we make. Neglect requires no effort, no energy and no decision. Actually, it does involve a decision: the decision not to make a decision.

OUR CHOICES DETERMINE OUR DESTINY

Our decisions make up our lives. Our choices determine our destiny. Our decisions should come out of our focus. You decide what you want and you focus on it. Then you continue to make decisions in keeping with your focus. Wrong decisions are a result of wrong input due to lack of focus or lack of clarity. Decision–making is all about taking responsibility for the direction of our lives.

The opposite of this is blame — trying to shift responsibility for whatever is not happening for us onto someone or something else. People who are constantly looking to blame someone or something else for the things that are wrong in their lives are actually only undermining what they are trying to build. We all have a tendency to do it at times. It's a basic tactic for avoiding responsibility. The reality is, though, that blame is never an effective strategy for progress. You never feel better just because you've shifted responsibility through blame. Blame chips away at what is valuable. It actually results in dishonour and fragmentation of what you are trying to build.

> *Wrong decisions are a result of wrong input*
> *due to lack of focus or lack of clarity*

So how do you learn to make right decisions? For a start, you need to learn to value the right things. You must make decisions based on an understanding of what is of value. In the absence of an understanding of value, you will always argue cost. A kilogram of rocks and a kilogram of diamonds weigh the same. Of course, diamonds are of much more value. But if you have no understanding of the relative value of rocks and diamonds, how would you know which to choose?

There is a direct relationship between what you value and how you spend your money. I was once in a bookstore with a friend buying a cookbook. (Being Italian, cooking is one of my passions.) I was at the sales desk paying for the book and it rang up at $129.95. My friend couldn't believe the price.

"How could you spend $130 on a cookbook?" he asked me incredulously.

I looked at him and said, "The guy who wrote this book has been a chef for 27 years. How much money do you think 27 years of experience is worth?"

As far as I was concerned, being able to buy the benefits of 27 years of cooking experience for only $129.95 was an absolute bargain! This particular book represented real value to me, so I was willing to pay the price asked in order to progress my own culinary ability. My friend saw no such value, so for him the book cost too much.

YOUR HEART IS WHERE YOUR TREASURE IS

How you spend your money determines what you value. If I value my time, I will spend money on things that will free up my time. If I value money, I will use my money to make more money. If I value my health, I will spend money on things like a gym membership and healthy food. If I value family, I will spend money on great holidays and other activities that create a happy family life. If I value my wife, I'll spend money on flowers and restaurants and gifts. As one of the world's great leaders once said, "Where your treasure is, there your heart will be also."

Once you determine what is valuable — what is a priority and what is irreplaceable in your life — you will make decisions accordingly. You'll even be prepared to take significant risks if it means pursuing something of value. In the book *Locking Arms*, Stu Webber relates a great story that illustrates this point. It's about two soldiers — Jim and Bill — who served together in the trenches during World War I and the deep friendship that developed between these two buddies serving together in the mud and the misery of that wretched conflict. Month after month they were stuck in a stalemate situation, pinned down in the cold and the mud of the trenches under constant fire. Every now and then, under orders from remote commands, one side or the other would rise out of the trenches and throw their bodies against the opposing line only to crawl back to the trenches to bury their dead and lick their wounds and wait until they had to do it all over again. In the midst of all this hopelessness and misery, Jim and Bill forged a strong bond. Day after day, night after night, terror after terror, they talked about their lives, their families and their hopes for the future.

Do your values drive your decision–making?

On one of these fruitless charges, Jim fell, severely wounded, while Bill made it back to the relative safety of the trenches. Jim lay suffering in 'no–man's–land' between the trenches, alone beneath the night flares. The shelling continued. The danger was at its peak. Bill was determined to reach his friend to rescue him from his awful predicament, but the commanding officer refused to let Bill leave the trench — it was simply too dangerous. While the CO's back was turned, however, Bill went over the top. Ignoring the smell of cordite in the air, the concussion of incoming rounds, and the pounding in his chest, Bill made it to Jim and somehow managed to get him back to the safety of the trenches. But it was too late — by the time Bill got him back, his friend was dead.

One self–righteous officer, seeing Jim's body, cynically asked Bill if it had been worth the risk. Bill's response was without hesitation: "Yes, Sir, it was," he said. "My friend's last words made it more than worth it. When I got to him, he looked up at me and said, 'I knew you'd come'." Bill had made a decision based on what he valued, no matter what the risk.

CHALLENGE

Are you prepared to make decisions based on what you value, no matter what the risk? What are the things that you really value? Do your values drive your decision–making? Do you have a clear sense of being in control of your life? Or do you let other people and circumstances make your decisions for you? Having a millionaire mindset means being a decisive person. Take charge of your world today — decide to decide.

CHAPTER 15

no one is an island

The great Olympic pole vaulter, Bob Richards, once said, "There is greatness all around you — welcome it! It is easy to be great when you get around great people."

To develop a millionaire mindset, you're going to need some help. (Presumably, you already know that, otherwise you wouldn't be reading this book!) We need role models in all areas of our lives: career, business, character, family, wealth — in everything that matters. There's an ancient proverb that says, "He who walks with the wise shall be wise." If you want to move ahead in life, you need to connect yourself to people who've done what you want to do, who've forged paths to prosperity that you can follow.

The company we keep can make or break us. As the saying goes, "If you want to fly with the eagles, don't hang out with the turkeys." When champion boxer Mike Tyson had Cus D'Amato as his coach, he was in a good place. He wasn't doing destructive things like hanging around gang members and thugs. He was living well and making good progress in life. Cus D'Amato did three key things for Mike Tyson: he helped him find a sense of belonging by taking him into his family, he helped him believe in himself, and he helped him to become something extraordinary.

YOU BECOME LIKE THOSE WITH WHOM YOU ASSOCIATE

If you want to increase and prosper in life, then you need to give attention to your associations. My father used to say to me, "Tell me who you walk with and I'll tell you who you'll become." Who are you hanging around with? If you are hanging around with small–minded, negative, complaining people, then you'll become like them. If you hang around positive, big thinking, 'can–do' people, you'll become like them.

Everybody needs three kinds of relationships:

1. People we look up to and follow — mentors, coaches and role models.
2. Peers with whom we can share our lives and to whom we can talk about deep issues.
3. People who are following us.

This is not about levels of superiority or inferiority; it's just a matter of different kinds of relationships and how they work. We need to get our philosophy of life from the first group, not the third group. You don't go to your kids for advice on how to raise them. The people you look up to are particularly important because they represent what you want to become and what you want to grow into. Many people don't have anyone in their lives like that.

The company we keep can make or break us.

I've been fortunate enough in my life to have had personal input from some of the great prosperity thinkers — people like Zig Ziglar, Robert Kiyosaki, Dennis Waitley, Brian Tracy and Stephen Covey, to name a few. How would you like that? Then do what I do. Get them in your car. And if you like something they say, push rewind and listen to it again!

When Mike Tyson was taking his direction from his coach, Cus D'Amato, all was well with him. He became the world's youngest heavyweight boxing champion. But when his level two and level three associations began to dictate his lifestyle and thought patterns, things went downhill. Who's influencing your thinking? Who are you allowing to speak into your world? Who's your coach? Who are your role models? Who are the people you are allowing to influence the way you think?

People often ask me whether I think anyone is born a leader. My answer is, "No, we're all born babies." Leadership is a learned art. Success is learned. Prosperity is learned. That's why we need teachers — people who stretch our thinking and help us grow. One of my close personal friends, a man who has helped me greatly in my life, is an owner of one of the largest tea and coffee franchises in Australia. In times of difficulty in my life he would repeatedly say to me, "Stand tall, Pat! Stand tall!" His encouragement and support have been critical to me at times. This is the kind of person you want as a friend — someone who will encourage you to think bigger, who will challenge you to grow, and who will believe in you.

YOUR ASSOCIATIONS MAKE YOU

Your associations build you. Your associations make you. As the great African American track star Wilma Rudolph once said, "No matter what great things you accomplish, somebody helps you." No matter how successful we become, we will always need other people to help us continue to progress. Even Tiger Woods spends time with a coach every day. Every level of success will bring you into higher associations. To get to a higher level of association, you sometimes have to stretch your comfort zone. Sometimes we can be afraid of going to another level because it might mean losing current associations and friends. The fact is, every new level of success will always bring us into a new level of relationships and associations.

> *Your associations build you. Your associations make you.*

Some time ago, I had the privilege of meeting the Prime Minister of Australia. I was attending a function with a whole lot of other people, including a number of my own friends and acquaintances. When I arrived, I found that I had been seated at a table with the Prime Minister and some other special guests. My friends were all seated at another table in another room. I have to admit, I felt uncomfortable meeting the Prime Minister. I was more comfortable with the status quo of being with people I knew. But I had to understand that to meet the Prime Minister, someone who operates at a higher level of leadership, influence and power, was an opportunity to be grasped. I knew I had to stretch myself to go outside my comfort zone. Once I decided to flow with the opportunity, it actually turned out to be a most enjoyable experience.

CHALLENGE

Think about the people in your own world and identify who is important to you. Who are your mentors and role models? Who are your most important peers — the people you can share your life with and who will support you, encourage you and believe in you? If you find that you are lacking meaningful associations, start identifying some people today that you think you need to get closer to and take whatever steps are necessary to build your connections with them.

CHAPTER 16

what's your dream?

Once during an interview, Paul McCartney was asked how he came to write his famous song *Yesterday.* "I dreamed it," he said. He actually woke up one morning with the tune in his head. As he ate breakfast that morning he put the following words to the tune: "Scrambled egg. How I love to eat a scrambled egg." Later he put a little more thought into the lyrics and the rest, as they say, is history.

I recently watched the great Australian champion fighter Kostya Tszyu lose a fight to UK boxer Ricky Hatton. I later learned that this had all started a long time ago. Tszyu had just won a world title fight and a young Hatton — who at the time had only had a few professional fights — jumped into the ring after the fight and said to Tszyu, "I have a dream that one day I'm going to fight you for the world title." That was his dream and now he has seen that dream fulfilled.

Nothing ever happens without a dream. People who do not have a dream about their future do not know where they are heading. But dreamers know where they are heading; they know where their future lies. They aim strategically and, like an arrow on target, they will hit their desired goal. Every great achievement begins with a dream. Henry Ford dreamt that lots of people could drive an affordable motor vehicle. Martin Luther King Jr changed an entire nation with the words, "I have a dream."

BEFORE ANYTHING SIGNIFICANT HAPPENS, IT ALWAYS STARTS WITH A DREAM

Dreams are a catalyst for releasing extraordinary achievements and prosperity. In 1982, at the official opening of the newly completed Epcot Center at Disney World in Florida, one of the Disney executives turned to Walt Disney's widow, Lillian, and said, "If only Walt could have seen this".

"He did," she replied, "That's why it's here."

Before anything significant is ever manifest, it always starts as a dream.

A dream is an intangible picture by which you create a tangible future. As Aristotle once said, "The soul cannot think without a picture." The extent of your prosperity will be constrained by the size of your dream. To develop a millionaire mindset, you need to become a big dreamer, a big thinker. David Schwartz said, "Where success is concerned, people are not measured in inches, or pounds, or college degrees, or family backgrounds. They are measured by the size of their thinking." As Donald Trump put it, "You have to think anyway, so why not think big?"

> *Dreams are a catalyst for releasing extraordinary achievements and prosperity.*

When someone like Jack Welch, the once great leader of General Electric, says that ongoing relationship with a customer is more important than the sale of an individual product, he is focusing on the big picture. What is the big picture in your area of work or business? Is it product, profitability or people? It may be none or all of those three. Understand what the big picture is, because it's the big picture that will create wealth and motivation.

Playwright Victor Hugo observed, "A small man is made up of small thoughts." To develop a millionaire mindset you have got to learn to think big — to have a big view of the world, a big view of life, a big view of yourself, and a big view of others. If you live with a small view of things, you are putting a lid on your progress and your prosperity.

A MILLIONAIRE MIND IS A MIND THAT DREAMS BIG

How big can you dream? What limitations are you putting on yourself, your prosperity and your wealth? A millionaire mind is a mind that dreams big. If the dream is big enough, the facts don't matter. The key to your prosperity lies in the seed of your dream. James Allen said, "Dreams are the seedlings of reality." There is nothing more powerful than a dream. Bestselling author Tom Clancy once said, "Nothing is as real as a dream." The world might change around you, but your dream remains constant. No matter what happens, no one can take your dream away from you as long as you stay determined to hold onto it.

A study conducted by Harvard physiologist David McClelland discovered that high achievers and successful people have one important common characteristic: they fantasise and dream incessantly about how to achieve their goals. Here are some examples:

- After his older brother was shot down and killed in World War II, Dick Clark would listen to the radio for hours to ease his painful loneliness. He began dreaming of someday becoming an announcer with his own radio show. The result of Clark's dream was the hugely successful show *American Bandstand.*

- Two brothers–in–law started their own business and advertised a single product served 31 different ways. Their dream was to make $75 a week. Today, the Baskin–Robbins ice cream company is a dream come true, not only for its founders, but also for ice cream lovers everywhere!

- The Bank of America exists today because A.P. Giannini, a high school drop–out, dreamed of starting a financial institution that served the little guy. By making unheard of automobile and appliance loans, his dream had become a reality by the time of his death in 1949.

- American cyclist Lance Armstrong dreamed that one day

he would win the Tour de France. At last count, he has won the famous event seven times!

- Walt Disney had a dream to build a theme park. What started as a scribbly little mouse went on to become one of the biggest and most successful entertainment empires in the world today.

IT COSTS NOTHING TO DREAM

It costs nothing to dream, but it will cost you not to have one. As Dr Robert Schuller said, "Since it doesn't cost a dime to dream, you should never short–change yourself when you stretch your imagination." Woodrow Wilson said:

> All big men are dreamers. They see things in the soft haze of a spring day or in the red fire of a long winter's evening. Some of us let these great dreams die, but others nourish and protect them; nurse them through bad days till they bring them to the sunshine and light which comes always to those who sincerely hope that their dreams will come true.

Between yesterday's dream and tomorrow's regret is today's opportunity. You need to capitalise on today's opportunities. Make the most of every opportunity that comes your way. See opportunities as the path to the fulfilment of your dream. Dreams must generate action, otherwise the dream will never become a reality. What actions can you take right now to cause your dreams to become reality?

> *See opportunities as the path to the fulfilment of your dream. Dreams must generate action, otherwise the dream will never become a reality.*

Of course, the whole point of having a dream is to see that dream fulfilled. Hyatt Resorts once had a slogan that said, "Having your dreams fulfilled can be more therapeutic than having them analysed." Don't spend your whole life analysing your dream — fulfil it! Don't let anyone else analyse your dream and tear it to bits. Don't expect anyone else to understand your dream — it is your dream, not theirs. Actor Kevin

Costner once said, "All of us as children have dreams and then our realities set in." You should never allow present day realities to kill your dream. Your dream is about your future, not your present. Don't allow so–called 'experts' to rob you of your dream.

A MILLIONAIRE MINDSET IS NOT SHAKEN BY THE NEGATIVE OPINIONS OF CRITICS

Many people will say to you, "It can't be done" or "You don't have what it takes" or "It has been tried before. What makes you think you can succeed where others have failed?" or "You're being too ambitious." Plenty of people will find reasons to dismiss your dream. The millionaire mindset is not shaken by the negative opinions of critics. For every major achievement in history, there would have been someone somewhere saying it couldn't be done, that it was impossible.

Let me say a few things about that word 'impossible'. It is a word that reflects a small mindset. To the millionaire mindset, 'impossible' is not a declaration — it's a dare. Impossible is an opinion. It does not have to be a fact. At the time John F. Kennedy announced that man would one day walk on the moon, it was technologically impossible to do it. But even though JFK never lived to see the fulfilment of the vision, that day he created a big picture in the thinking of the American people and the impossible became possible. At one stage they said it was impossible to run the mile in under four minutes. Today you could not even qualify for the Olympics if you can't run a mile under four minutes. By declaring something 'impossible', somebody with a small mindset dares someone else to live in the big picture.

Instead of listening to the critics and the sceptics, hang around the dreamers. I love to hang around people who dream. We just hang around, drink coffee, talk about anything and everything… and dream.

YOUR DREAM DETERMINES YOUR BEHAVIOUR

You must believe the dream. To grow into reality, an extraordinary dream must be fed. Your dream should determine your conduct and behaviour. Your dream should lead you to make appointments that will foster the fulfilment of the dream. Your dream will give birth to changes in your relationships and brand new habits for success and wealth. Dreams are generally birthed by a deep desire for change, for something to be better than it is. Your dream will give birth to extraordinary passion that dominates your consciousness and thoughts.

Although dreams are free, the fulfilment of a dream will require sacrifice. Look at anyone who has ever dreamed and seen their dream fulfilled and you'll see that it has always cost them something. Martin Luther King Jr had a dream, but it cost him his life. It may cost you friendship, it may cost you a change of thinking, it may cost you a whole lot of things, but any dream worth pursuing is worth paying the price.

It's amazing how many people allow their dreams to be shattered just because they face a few challenges or obstacles. We all have challenges. We all have issues. I know I have issues! Here's a fact of life: right now you are either leaving a crisis or about to enter one. "When is it all going to stop?" you may ask. When you're dead! The fulfilment of dreams involves heartaches, struggles and challenges. That's what makes it so worthwhile when you achieve your dream.

I remember how at the age of 17 I got a vision for my life. I didn't even fully understand it at the time. All I could see was a sea of faces of young people and I knew I would one day be speaking into their lives. I heard a little voice inside me say, "You can build this." I remember going to a youth convention that was so boring that even boring people called it boring! And I looked at it and thought, "I could take over this one day and make it better!" A little voice inside me said, "Good!" I remember they had a terrible choir at this youth convention and I thought, "The first thing I'll do is sack the choir." And again the voice said, "Good!"

MONEY FOLLOWS VISION

Some time later, I started my first event with a crowd of 350 young people and no budget. I have found in life that lack of money is never really the problem — lack of vision is the problem. I've never had enough money to do the things I wanted. But I've found that money follows vision. If you don't have the money, it simply means the vision isn't big enough.

After my first event, I lost about 180 people because they didn't agree with what I was doing. But I had a vision. I knew what I wanted to do. At my next event I had 300 people, then 500, then 800, then 1,000, then 1,200... Soon I was packing the Sydney Town Hall. Then we packed out Sydney's 5,000–seat Hordern Pavilion, then the State Sports Centre which holds 7,000. Next, I set my sights on the 12,000–seat Sydney Entertainment Centre. I remember people saying to me, "Where are you going to get the money for that?"

"Well, obviously not from you!" was my reply.

You see, money's never the problem — vision is. I remember one day walking into the empty Sydney Entertainment Centre and saying to myself, "I'm going to fill this building." I went on to fill it seven times.

I had more young people turning up to my events than at most rock concerts. After that, I went to the Parramatta Football Stadium, a large outdoor sports arena in the heart of Sydney. People were still asking me, "Where will you get the money? How will you do it?" To be honest, I didn't have a clue. We can be too dependent on clues. Sometimes our problem is that we think we need to know exactly how it is going to be done instead of believing in our dream and in ourselves. Sometimes you just have to have a go. You just have to go out and do it.

DETERMINE TO FOLLOW YOUR DREAM

Follow the dream. Follow your heart and your vision. As much as we need to have a plan, we can spend too much time sitting around analysing and over–planning. What is ultimately important is the dream and the vision. So when the plan fails or things don't go according to plan, the vision is still alive. It's the vision, not the plan, that keeps us going. I love that old Elvis song that says, "I'm going to follow that dream." You may ask, "What happens if it doesn't work?" But what if it does? What would happen if even 20 percent of your dream came to pass?

Without a dream or a vision you will get to the end of your life and wonder what could have been. Everybody ends up somewhere in life. You can either end up somewhere on purpose or just end up wherever you allow life to take you. If you don't have a vision for your life, then you will have no control over your destination. How do you want to be remembered after you're gone? You don't want written on your gravestone, "She kept a clean house." What do you want on your gravestone? "Here lies a shoulda, coulda, woulda…" What do you want said about your life? One day, these words could describe your legacy: "Here lies a dreamer. He dared to dream!"

> *If you don't have a vision for your life, then you will have no control over your destination.*

In 1866, Alfred Nobel invented dynamite as a result of trying to make nitroglycerine safer to handle. Although he hadn't invented dynamite with a view to it being used in warfare, this soon became the case. Nobel later became involved in the development of weaponry, but he also maintained an ideological commitment to peace. It has been said that the reason he instituted the Nobel Peace Prize was that he wanted his primary legacy to the world to be the promotion of peace, not war.

When people have no vision for the future, they tend to do three things:

- They revert to their past.
- They spend all their time making excuses for why their lives are going nowhere.
- They stop living and settle for merely existence.

When I was running my drug rehabilitation program, many of the boys who were resident in our program had no real vision for their lives beyond getting out of the program. All they wanted to do was to get clean and quit drugs. Human nature is such that unless a person has a clear picture of their future, they will always return to their past. While these boys had no vision for their futures, I could pretty much guarantee that even if they left our program clean, it would only be a matter of time before they reverted back into their old habits.

CHALLENGE

What's your dream? What do you see in your future? Don't focus on where you are right now. You need to see beyond what is now to what could be and what should be. All of us should have a vision for our wealth, for our health, for our families, for the people we can influence, and for our businesses or careers. What is in your heart of hearts? What is the thing that you long to do in your wildest dreams? How big is it? How big can you make this thing called 'your life'?

If you don't have a dream for your life, someone else will have one for you. When I was a kid, my father used to say to me, "Son, when you get bigger, you're going to be a doctor." So I never got bigger! And anyway, that wasn't my dream, it was my father's dream. Some of us can easily be carried along by other people's dreams — including our partner's dream — but it's your dream, not theirs, that is important. No one should ever rob you of your dream, especially if they love you. If someone really loves you, then they'll love everything about you, including your dreams that they may not really understand or agree with. If they truly love you, they should say, "Well, if that makes you happy, if that's what you want to do, I'll support you, I'll help you make it happen."

To escape the past, you need to create your future today… and it starts with a dream. Stephen Covey says, "Begin with the end in mind." Without a vision for your future, you'll reach the end of your life and look back and wonder what could have been if things had been different. You will find yourself always talking about the 'good old days' and regretting what you might have become. There is nothing more tragic than hearing someone in their latter years utter the words, "if only…" And there is nothing more inspiring than seeing a person near the end of their life able to look back and declare, "I did it! I finished the race. I achieved what I set out to achieve."

What will you be saying at the end of your life? What is your vision for the next year, two years, five years, and 10 years? Your future has to start as a picture in your head today. What's your vision? How will your dream come true?

CHAPTER 17

dreams are fuelled by passion

There is no such thing as emotionless vision. Even the most lifeless, routine activities feel good when you have a dream. It's all about passion. I'm Italian — I was born with passion! I get passionate and emotional about everything. I'd cry at the opening of a supermarket! Robert Kiyosaki defines passion as the tension that exists between something you love and something you hate. I'm passionate about seeing people become wealthy. I love seeing people prosperous and succeeding in life. I hate seeing people broke and struggling to get by. My passion is the tension I feel between these things…between the things I love and the things I hate.

Passion involves a tension between two things: as much as you love a thing, you also hate its opposite. To be passionate about prosperity, you have to hate poverty. The tension you feel between these two positions is passion.

You have to get emotional about your dream. You have to feel something. I get emotional about drug addiction. I don't believe in harm minimisation because it doesn't work. I remember a time when I had to confront a very senior political figure in my home state about the issue of drug addiction and I was spitting mad. He could see it in my eyes. I was running a drug rehabilitation program with an 86 percent success rate and they were opening shooting galleries for drug addicts. I couldn't believe it! I was so mad. But I directed my anger toward a positive and productive end by deciding to prove them wrong. I also get passionate about young kids being dealt antidepressants at six and seven years of age. As far as I'm concerned, that's wrong. Maybe they just need a friend. I get passionate about shifting people's mindsets away from poverty to prosperity. I find myself thinking, "If you could just see what I see."

THE SOUL CAN'T THINK WITHOUT A PICTURE

Do you get emotional about what you believe in? Do you get emotional about your wealth? Do you get emotional about your business? Are you emotionally attached to what you do? You cannot be emotionally detached from what you do and expect to be successful. Your soul is the seat of your emotions. Remember Aristotle's dictum: the soul can't think without a picture. The picture in your soul should stir you emotionally. It's like when you are in love with someone and that person isn't present, but you can see them in your mind's eye. If there's no emotion attached to your dream, it remains lifeless. When someone is passionate about what they do, their passion rubs off on the people around them. The difference between being bored and excited by something someone is telling you has less to do with your interest in the subject than it has to do with how passionate that person is about what they're telling you.

I'll say it again: dreams and vision have to involve emotion. The clearer and stronger your vision is, the stronger your emotion will be. As teenagers, we fall in and out of love all the time and there is always a certain amount of emotion attached to that. But when you find the person that you want to spend the rest of your life with, the emotion becomes a lot stronger because the vision in front of you is clearer and more long–term.

VISION IS ALWAYS EMOTIONAL

When it comes to developing a millionaire mindset, you have to love your dream and love what you are doing to make your dream a reality. If you don't love what you are doing, then do something else! Vision is always emotional. Everyone has a different vision because everyone gets excited by different things. I have friends who have a great vision for their computer business. I have no vision for computers — I don't even like the things! But when my friends speak about their computers and technology and what they can do, it is almost as though they are speaking about the person that they want to spend the rest of their life with. (Unfortunately, most of us *do* spend too much time with our computers!) They are passionate about their vision. It stirs them, it enthuses them, and it motivates them.

There is usually a strong correlation between what you are passionate about and what you are good at. That means your prosperity is more than likely going to flow out of your strengths and gifts. You'll never create wealth out of projects you're not good at or projects you don't enjoy. I've yet to meet a wealthy person who got wealthy doing stuff they don't enjoy. If you don't enjoy what you're doing in your business or your work right now, you probably won't become prosperous doing that. You can't have two diametrically opposed thoughts about the same thing and expect to be successful. Surveys have found that 70 to 80 percent of people hate their jobs. A similar percentage of people are in the wrong career because it doesn't match their abilities and preferences. If you don't enjoy the job you're in right now, it's highly unlikely that you'll ever become wealthy from it. My advice is to do something else. It's often said, "Find a job you love and you'll never have to work another day in your life."

> *Your prosperity is more than likely going to flow out of your strengths and gifts.*

I know I will never get wealthy doing administrative work or developing computer programs. I don't know a thing about them and I have no passion for these things. Singing is not my gift either. I was driving with my wife one day and Michael Bolton came on the radio singing 'How Am I Supposed to Live Without You?' So I started singing this song to Andrea and she said, "Shut up or you'll find out!" My gift is speaking, teaching, inspiring and motivating people. There are days when I get tired of doing what I do, but I love what I do. I love speaking. I really enjoy it.

(Whether people love listening to me is another matter!) I love creating books and CDs and putting them into people's hands and saying, "Okay, go get rich!"

CREATE WEALTH FROM YOUR POSITION OF STRENGTH

What is your gift? You will create prosperity out of your gifting. You will always create wealth from your position of strength. How many times have you heard someone tell you that you need to figure out your gift and work on your weaknesses? What a load of nonsense! Michael Jordan was a great basketball player who retired from basketball to try his hand at baseball. But no matter how much he focused on baseball, he was never going to be great. On the basketball court, though, he was a superman. If the Bulls were down by two points with only five seconds to go, the coach would call time out and no matter what instructions he might have been giving the team, everybody knew that there was one guy who was going to get the ball — Michael Jordan. Focus on your gift. Don't expect prosperity to come from outside of your area of giftings. Work on your strengths instead.

Vision has to involve passion and motivation. You can always identify motivated people because they are passionate. *The Collins Dictionary* defines passion as 'eagerness, excitement, fervour, fire, heat, intensity, rapture, joy, spirit, zest and zeal'. Does that describe how you feel about creating prosperity in your life? Does that describe how you feel about the vision you have for your life?

Passion is not nebulous; it is always directed at something. It is generally directed at a vision of how things can and should be. Vision is born out of concern. What stirs you up? What moves you? What drives you to action? For many years I have been passionate about helping people become self–managed and self–motivated. I am passionate about helping people discover and release their capacity to create wealth. Why? Because I believe in the power of free enterprise. I am passionate about being a compassionate capitalist! In other words, I have prosperity for a purpose. My money, your money, our money can accomplish great things. With money, we can make the world a better place.

PASSION IS BORN OUT OF CONCERN

All my passion is born out of concern for something. I am even passionate about food – especially Italian food! I become greatly disturbed and concerned when people don't cook Italian food the way it ought to be cooked! Some time ago I was at one of my favourite Italian restaurants in Sydney. The owner, who recently celebrated his 50th year in business, told me how he had recently been to another Italian restaurant in another state. His words were, "How could they cook food like that?" He was disgusted at how some Italian restaurants produce the great dishes that come from Italy. He was passionate because he was concerned; passion and concern are two sides of the same coin.

> *But a dream can transform even the most tedious and repetitive task into purposeful, goal–directed activities.*

When your dream is infused with passion, even the most mundane aspects of fulfilling your dream become meaningful. Everybody has to do mundane things on a day–to–day basis. No dream becomes a reality without a considerable amount of routine, menial work. But a dream can transform even the most tedious and repetitive task into purposeful, goal–directed activities.

Imagine that you work in a factory that produces sandbags. Imagine if all you had to do all day, every day, was fill bags with sand. Imagine how boring that would be. Now imagine that your home and everything you own is under threat from rising flood waters and the only way you can save your home is by building walls with bags of sand. Under those circumstances, filling sandbags would become your obsession. You'd throw everything you had into it. What's the difference? The difference is that now your emotions are engaged and you have a vision — to see your home survive the flood. Vision gives significance to the mundane. You do whatever you have to do to get you to where you want to go. You do it with enthusiasm because it is all about fulfilling your personal dream.

One of the things I find mundane is flying. I really hate flying, whatever class of ticket I might have. But when I get to my destination, it's a different story. I'm thinking about who might be in the meeting. It could be the next Bill Gates. There could be someone there who is going to change the world. I remember one day a man invited me to come and speak at an event he had organised with about 7,000 people attending. When I got to the event, I was impressed.

"Who inspired you to do this?" I asked him.

"You did," he said.

I was surprised. "But I've never met you before," I said.

"Yes, you have," he replied. "I was at a youth camp years ago and you were the speaker. I came up to you during the camp and asked you, 'How can I build a big organisation like you have?' And you looked at me and said, 'Son, get a dream and work your butt off.' And that's what I did. And that's why I wanted you to be the speaker at my first big event."

MUNDANE TASKS ARE MANDATORY TO YOUR SUCCESS

Recently I was working with a group of real estate professionals and I asked them to identify one of the most mundane activities that they had to do in the course of their jobs. Someone replied, "Answering the phone." Now, I would have thought that answering the phone is quite important in real estate, as in any business. I pointed out that one of the great lessons in sales success is, 'If I don't ring, my phone doesn't ring.' Another basic axiom of business is, 'When the phone rings, answer it.' It may seem a mundane task, but it is mandatory to your success and the profitability of your organisation. That makes it meaningful.

Of course, the potential downside of being passionate is that it leaves you open to disappointment when things don't go according to plan. If there's no passion, you rarely get disappointed because you don't really care. But when you care, you can experience the downside of passion. All of us have disappointments in our lives. The answer is to ensure that your vision always exceeds your disappointment quota. If your disappointment quota exceeds your vision quota, then your disappointment will overtake your vision.

How do you ensure your vision quota always stays above your disappointment quota? It's largely a matter of managing expectations.

Disappointment comes from unmet expectations. Don't get disappointed with yourself by putting unreasonable expectations on yourself. I expect a high standard of myself in a lot of areas, but I also know there are some things I'm not good at, so I don't put unrealistic expectations on myself in those areas. I don't allow myself to be disappointed about certain things. Above all, you have to keep believing — no matter what. You have to believe that dreams come true.

CHALLENGE

What are you concerned about? What flicks your switch? What makes you angry? What makes you exuberant? What makes you feel a sense of drive? What makes you burn with fervour? This is not about feelings, this is a disposition you need to have. You need to develop a passionate disposition about creating wealth for yourself and for others.

CHAPTER 18

the 'why' factor

Every vision needs to have a 'Why' factor. *Why* do you want to prosper? What's your ultimate motivation? My firm belief is that we need to have an ultimate purpose bigger than ourselves. Our passion needs to be directed outward to other people. If the only thing we are passionate about is ourselves, then our desire for prosperity is nothing more than an expression of a selfish narcissism. Ultimately, your pursuit of wealth needs to be altruistically motivated. Your over–arching attitude should not be "What's in it for me?" but "What's in it for them?" You need to ask yourself, "What value am I to others?" Go for a win–win every time — if you win, I win!

My own passion is born out of a general concern for humanity, specifically a concern for broken people. I am passionate about helping those who have no voice to discover a voice for themselves. I am passionately opposed to drug abuse. I am passionate about my friends' success. I am concerned that people should not have to rely on welfare to survive in the future. We must have a vision to create our own wealth. That's the 'Why' factor.

We need to understand that our success is linked to the success of the people around us. No one ever becomes a millionaire by themselves. If I can make life better for other people, it will make my life better. And if I can help the people around me become successful, then their success becomes my success. In a very real way, my income is the direct result of how many people I help. If the number one motivation in your life is to accept responsibility for adding value to the lives of other people, everything else will fall into place.

NO ONE EVER ACHIEVED SUCCESS WITHOUT THE HELP OF OTHERS

Thomas J. Stanley relates the story of Coach Paul "Bear" Bryant, a highly successful and respected US college football coach. At a seminar for senior executives, Stanley asked one of Coach Bryant's former players the following question: "What was the first thing Coach Bryant said to you and the other scholarship athletes after you arrived on campus?" The player said that Coach Bryant's first words had taken everyone by surprise: "Have you called your folks yet to thank them?" While everyone was still trying to process the implications of this, Coach Bryant followed up his question with another statement: "No one ever got to this level without the help of others. Call your folks. Thank them."

> *In a very real way, my income is the direct result of how many people I help.*

When actor Paul Newman and his friend A.E. Hotchner started their famous 'Newman's Own' brand of salad dressings and other products in 1978, they made a commitment to donate all the profits from the enterprise to charity. The company donated over one million dollars in its first year of operation. In the next 20 years they donated more than $125 million to a range of charities and aid organisations.

THE MILLIONAIRE MINDSET FOCUSES ON THE 'WHY' OF SUCCESS

A true millionaire mindset is always focused on the 'why' of success, and that often revolves around the needs of other people. A few years ago, I was helping out a youth program in Eastern Europe. One night I was out buying some 'McFood' for some of the kids and I saw one young man take his burger, cut it in half, wrap one half in his serviette and put it in his pocket. I said to him, "Hey, buddy! You don't have to hang on to that. We can buy some more burgers later." He replied that it wasn't for him, it was for his sister who hadn't eaten in days. Despite his own hunger, his first impulse was to share. His sister didn't know he had a burger, so she would have been none the wiser if he'd eaten the whole thing. But he put his sister's need before his own. That's a millionaire mindset.

You have probably heard the old saying, 'Give and it shall be given to you.' Most of us would rightly agree that giving is a virtuous act. The prosperous person is a giver. But the prosperous person also knows how to receive. You can only give away what you have already received. We need to become transmitters of wealth. A transmitter receives input and then transmits it out. In the same way, we need to be able to receive before we can give. The poor can't help the poor because they are poor. It is the prosperous person, the person of abundance, the flourishing person who can be a transmitter of wealth. But to become this kind of person, you have got to first learn to be a receiver.

Once you decide to be a receiver, it's amazing what you will attract. You will attract what you are willing to receive. Some people constantly attract trouble because they are willing to receive it. In all my years of working in drug rehabilitation and working with young people, even though drugs were around me everywhere, I have never been offered drugs — except once in Hawaii. Because I choose not to receive that environment around me, I don't attract it. Trouble can be everywhere around me, but I choose not to receive it. What are you choosing to receive? What are you allowing into your life that you don't want? Some people receive negativity and gossip all the time because they choose to receive these things. I choose not to. You need to develop your capacity to receive the things you want to receive into your life. When you receive compliments, do you put on false humility or do you receive it with thanks? When you receive money, do you feel like you need to apologise for it or feel bad about it? If you do, then you are putting a lid on your prosperity. These responses reflect a sense of unworthiness. When you receive wealth, you need to be comfortable with it — embrace it, acknowledge it and enjoy it.

How much you can receive is limited by how 'big' you are. A jar can contain only so much. A house can only contain so much. But a warehouse can contain so much more. To be a bigger receiver, you need a bigger capacity. The artist James Baillie said, "To grow and know what one is growing towards — that is the source of all strength and confidence in life." To grow and know that I am growing towards being a receiver with a capacity for prosperity brings a strength and dignity to my life that I can never have with a limited mindset.

To be a bigger receiver, you need a bigger capacity.

Everyone who believes in himself, no matter who he is, stands on a higher level and has a greater capacity than a person who is unsure of who he is and what he believes in. To be a receiver means you will stand out. To be prosperous means you will live at a higher level. The great Presbyterian minister William J.H. Boetcker said this:

> It has always been a crime to be above the crowd. That's the real reason why some in public life are maligned, attacked and slandered, for they are beyond the reach of those who realise in their own heart that the greatness of others shows their own smallness and their own inferiority.

DON'T LET YOUR PROSPERITY BE HINDERED BY OTHER PEOPLE'S SMALL MINDEDNESS

Never let your prosperity be hindered by other people's inferiority and small–mindedness. Never let other people hinder your capacity to receive. Your capacity to receive will always show up the smallness and limitations of others. As Ralph Waldo Emerson said, "To be great is to be misunderstood." If you desire prosperity and increase, you will be misunderstood. People who are going nowhere, doing nothing and achieving little are left alone, but once you choose to flourish, abound, increase and prosper, you face attack from all directions — from friends, colleagues and especially those who have no capacity to receive.

The Greyhound bus company used to have a motto: "When dealing in basic human need you will always be needed." If you want to be wealthy, you should focus your vision on dealing in basic human need. When our purpose is to meet needs, we are living for something beyond ourselves. How are you meeting needs in the lives of others? What are you doing to help other people belong, to be financially secure, and to have a sense of achievement? If you can deal in these three basic human needs, if your vision is to help people belong and be accepted, be financially secure and find a sense of achievement, then you are on your way to developing a millionaire mindset.

If you are meeting human needs, then all you have to do is help people to see that you are meeting their need. The reason people are prepared to pay me to do what I do is because I am meeting a need in them. If I wasn't meeting some need, then no matter how clever or articulate I might be, no one would want to hear from me.

SUCCESSFUL PEOPLE CARE ABOUT THE NEEDS OF OTHERS

A worthwhile vision will always show care and concern for people. Any great visionary is a person who cares about other people and their needs. In the USA, there's a department store called Nordstrom. A friend of mine took me there one day. He said, "Pat, you need to come and experience Nordstrom. Talk about customer service — you won't believe it. I'm going to take this pair of shoes back."

I said, "You're kidding! But you're wearing them!"

He said, "That's right. And I'm taking them back. They'll give me another pair of shoes, no questions asked."

We walked into the store and approached the sales desk. My friend explained that the shoes were not fitting well and that he wanted to exchange them for a new pair. (The shoes were worth about $400.) The sales assistant's immediate reply was, "Yes, sir. No problem at all." He then looked up my friend's customer details — including his shoe size — and asked if he would like another pair of black shoes. My friend decided he would prefer a brown pair. So the assistant went back to the storeroom and came out with a new pair of brown shoes. My friend tried them on and was happy. The assistant thanked him for his custom. "Always a pleasure to serve you, Mr Smith," he said.

As we left the store, I said to my friend, "Do you always bring your old shoes back here and get a new pair?"

"No," he replied. "I just wanted to show you what a great store this is. I always buy all my clothes at Nordstrom because their policy is that the customer always comes first and they mean it."

One day, a 'bag lady' — unwashed, smelly and shabbily dressed — walked into one of the big Nordstrom stores and went straight to a department that sold very expensive dresses. She walked up to a sales assistant and said, "I want to buy a dress. Not just any dress — I want a nice one. I'm going to a party and I want a nice dress to wear. I have money, you know."

The sales assistant politely replied, "No problem, ma'am. What size are you?"

"I don't know," the woman said.

So the assistant took her to a fitting area and measured her up and then began bringing her dresses worth $500, $800, and $1,500 for her to try on. Eventually she picked one she liked and the sales assistant asked, "Would you like some shoes to go with that?"

"Yes," the woman replied. "I do need shoes. And not just some cheap shoes — I'm going to a party and I want to look nice. I have money, you know."

So the assistant helped her out of her boots and came back with several pairs of expensive shoes. The assistant fitted her and helped her select a pair. The assistant then went on to help her select some nice jewellery to go with her outfit. Then she said, "Why don't we do something with your hair as well?"

The woman's hair was unwashed and matted. So the assistant took her to the hairdressing department and they washed her hair, cut it and put it up in a bun. When they were finished, the assistant showed the woman a mirror and said, "There, don't you look lovely?"

The woman looked at herself and replied, "Take it all off. I don't like it."

So they took everything off. She left without buying a thing. But before she left the store, the assistant gave her a card and said, "Thank you for visiting us here at Nordstrom today. It was a pleasure serving you. This is my name and my number. If you ever have any needs that I can help with, please feel free to call me at any time."

A few weeks later, an article appeared in a major US newspaper entitled, 'My experience at Nordstrom'. The bag lady had been an undercover reporter who had gone to the store to test whether their commitment to customer service lived up to the promise. That sales assistant became very popular on the speaking circuit. She became quite wealthy as a result of the way in which she had performed that day. When you treat people well, it unlocks the potential for wealth. People bring you money. But your vision must have at its core the wellbeing of other people.

CHALLENGE

So, *why* do you want to prosper? What ultimately motivates you? What is your purpose for success? You need to have an ultimate purpose bigger than yourself. If you don't have a purpose, go and search for one. Without a purpose, your passion will wane.

Here's my challenge to you: whatever you want, give it away — it will come back to you. If you want love, give love. If you want happiness, give happiness. If you want money, give it away. "But if I give it away, I won't have any left," you may say. Well, no. It's like a seed. There's a law in life called the law of seedtime and harvest. It's a universal law that has always been around and always will. According to this law, if you sow something of value, it will grow and return to you in increased measure. Focus on others, and others will focus on you.

CONCLUSION

I started this book by saying that I'm on a mission to help make people rich. I want to help make you rich, but first you've got to adopt a millionaire mindset. There is a reason why the rich get richer and the poor get poorer. Generally it has to do with mindsets. Some scientists once created a scenario in which all the wealth of the world was distributed equally amongst everybody. In other words, in this scenario you and I would have received a share of Bill Gates' money! The conclusion they came to was that every time they performed this scenario, over a short period of time the wealth would always return to the original owners. Why? Because the rich have a mindset that the poor don't have.

One of the early pioneers of Christianity, the apostle Paul, once wrote, "Do not conform any longer to the pattern of this world, but be transformed by the renewing of your mind."[5] That's essentially what this book is all about. Do not allow yourself to go through life simply conforming to the patterns of thinking and living that are dictated to you by the world around you. You could easily blame your upbringing, your education, negative social norms, or statements that may have been said about you. How should you respond? My friend, transform your life by the renewal of your mind.

[5] Romans 12:2 (New International Version)

In the 1979 film *Being There*, the late Peter Sellers played the main character: a gardener named Chance who had lived his entire life in an old mansion in the middle of Washington DC. Chance had never been outside the owner's property, spending every day tending the small walled garden attached to the house. Apart from limited contact with an African American housekeeper who came to the house each day to cook and clean, his only knowledge of the outside world was based on what he had seen on television, which he watched almost continually. When the owner of the mansion died, for the first time in his life, Chance had to leave the only home he had ever known and venture out into the outside world. The rest of the film is about how Chance survived in this big new world, interpreting and responding to every situation in which he found himself by relating it to what he had seen on television or to his knowledge of gardening.

The final line of the film is, "Life is a state of mind." While that sentiment might be a little too existentialist for me, it is certainly true to say that the path of your life will be determined to a large extent by the state of your mind. Remember, if there's a mist in your mind, there will be a fog surrounding your world.

So, as you begin today to change your mindset, the mist in your mind will begin to clear. And as the mist clears, the fog surrounding your world will lift ever so gently. As that happens, you'll find yourself beginning to see further than you've ever seen before. New horizons of opportunity and possibility will appear before you. Paths of prosperity that once eluded you now stretch out before you. Rivers of riches now flow within your reach. Gardens of greatness are now at your fingertips. With the dawn of each new day, you'll awake to the realisation that your dreams are achievable.

My friend, the difference between yesterday and today is simply that you decided to apply a millionaire mindset. And that has made all the difference!